In A Nutshell

LARRY F. CRACKS THE SECRETS OF EVERYDAY LIFE!

Larry Fedoruk

Stoddart

Published in 1998 by Stoddart Publishing Co. Limited
34 Lesmill Road, Toronto, Canada M3B 2T6
Tel. (416) 445-3333   Fax (416) 445-5967
Email customer.service@ccmailgw.genpub.com

02 01 00 99 98 1 2 3 4 5

Canadian Cataloguing in Publication Data

Fedoruk, Larry
In a nutshell: Larry F. cracks the secrets of everyday life

ISBN 0-7737-6005-9

1. Canadian wit and humor (English).*
2. In a nutshell (Radio program).
I. Title

PN 1991.3.C3F42 1998   C818'.5402   C97-931457-X

Cover Design: Bill Douglas @ The Bang
Text Design: Tannice Goddard

Printed and bound in Canada

*We gratefully acknowledge the Canada Council for the Arts and
the Ontario Arts Council for their support of our publishing program.*

Contents

Contents

Preface

Preface

"The born journalist knows 'that nothing under the sun is uninteresting.' Whatever he does — catching a cold, cutting a finger — he is impressed anew by the 'interestingness of mundane phenomena.' Most people find life dull. It is the journalist's job to make them see it is not, and for this the journalist must be gifted with the 'inexhaustible appreciative wonder of a child.'"
— JOHN CAREY OF THE *GLOBE AND MAIL*, CITING ARNOLD BENNETT IN *THE INTELLECTUALS AND THE MASSES*

I am not trying to pass off my "nutshells" as journalism; however, I have kept the above quote pinned up near my desk for the last few years as some sort of credo.

A couple of years ago the General Manager of CISS-FM in Toronto, Sharon Taylor, suggested that I do a daily editorial, some sort of humorous essay on how I see things. "Larry F. in a Nutshell" was the result.

You see, I am consumed, sometimes even obsessed, with the minutiae of living. This can be both a blessing and a curse. *In a Nutshell* stresses the importance of the "little things" that make up life itself. I truly believe these things to be important, and I have blessed and cursed the opportunity to talk about them daily on the radio. Now, with this

▷ X ◁

book, you have the opportunity to do so as well. I hope you enjoy it. Together, we can wade through the immense details that are daily living.

Currently, my mother, my brother Gregg, and my children, Kelly and Steven, provide me with a tremendous appreciation for the everyday. I thank them for that now and always. And of course I thank my friend Sharon Taylor, who shares the fascination, and who gave me the push needed to get this done.

John Lennon said, "Life is what happens while you're busy making other plans." In this book I look at the little things that happen. Maybe, while planning your life, you can take a moment to enjoy them. I do. I really do.

Larry Fedoruk
June 1998

Be a

Sport

Body Building

I don't know if I understand body building. I'm not talking about getting in shape or having nice muscle tone. I'm talking about massive, competitive, little Speedo bathing suit, flex-until-you-have-this-pained-look body building. What's it about? How is it attractive?

Sure, women want nice legs and small waists, and men want large chests and flat stomachs. If that's your goal and you can do it, great. But at what point does a person decide that they want the world's biggest tri-flebuloid spartacus plexatator? Have you ever watched one of these body building competitions on TV? They're talking about working body parts you've never even heard of. It's the same thing if you've ever tried to join a health club.

"Work the tone of your glutes."

"Work your own glutes, pal . . . and I don't like your tone."

I've tried to keep up and I can't. These body builders become like cult leaders and I always try and pretend like I know what I'm talking about.

"What are you working today, Larry?"

"Well, today I thought I'd work on my Lexus, my Serbo-Croatia, my Tyrannosaurus rex, and my Mesopotamia. Tomorrow, I'm working on my AC Delco, my pictorials, and my Vasco De Gama!"

Who cares, really? I'm trying to stay in some shape and live past fifty. I don't want to be a body builder. For one thing, those guys wear T-shirts twelve months a year. They must freeze in winter. After all that body work, they want to show it off. And now the women are so pumped up. I don't want to look at a woman and the first thing I think of is, "She could crush me like a twig." I don't think women want to think that about a man either.

Putting on as few clothes as possible, oiling yourself up, and going on stage is against the law in most cities. Call it body building and all a the sudden, it's a sport. Hey, unless you're posing for a superhero comic book, stop pumping up — pump down. I don't care what you say, it can't be healthy. Mind you, I wouldn't mind a nice, big Lexus.

Golfing To Meet People

They say golf is a great way to meet people. This is the biggest myth of the sport. People you meet on the golf course talk about nothing *but* golf. You can spend four hours with someone and not only not remember their name, but know absolute diddly about them.

Sure, you make an effort. "So, Kevin, uh, Frank, Bob, whatever, what do you do?"

"Well, I'm a nuclear physicist, I just landed the space shuttle, and after my messy divorce from Claudia Schiffer, I invented a cure for all diseases."

"Really . . . hey, did you see that shot Tiger made at the Masters on the 16th? Oh yeah, that was good, oh yeah, good, good."

As an iffy golfer, I generally meet only two kinds of people on the course: those who know everything about golf and feel the need to share it with me, and those who know nothing at all about golf and feel the need to share it with me. The latter are my favourite.

"Gee, it looks like your shot went too far right, looks like your putt was a little short. Ooooo, that one bounced too far." Yes, I know. Shut up.

The others, the experts, really don't help at all either. You think you're doing okay, until finally one of them breaks down, bursting with the knowledge that's been bundled up inside.

"You know if you just went back on your heels a little more, widened your stance, bent your left knee, dropped your shoulder, came back straighter, tucked in your chin, moved your top hand, loosened your grip, stiffened that wrist, swung through a little more . . ."

"Well, if you just closed your mouth, walked to your car, found the keys, drove home, and never bothered me again . . ." Boy, it's a relaxing game, isn't it?

Golf: It's terrible exercise, the game drives you crazy, it takes at least four hours out of your day, but oh, the people you meet!

Camping

Every May long weekend, I'm reminded that campers are better people than me.

I've always wanted to be a camper — a hearty soul with big boots and a woolly shirt, a friend to the bear and the beaver, in harmony with nature, at one with the sun and the wind. Perched on a rock by a steamy lake, watching the sunrise with a cup of chicory-laced coffee in my hand. This is the person I've wanted to be, the person I thought I could be, the person I've tried to be many times, but failed.

I'm not good with camping. To me, camping is missing the one key ingredient to a good vacation: room service. And hey, here's a new business idea for you for the next century, provide camping room service for upper-middle-class yuppie campers. Go ahead, it's yours. I'm giving you the idea free of charge.

I like all the individual elements of camping. I like the outdoors. Tents are cozy, sleeping bags are romantic, food cooked over an open flame is tasty. But combine two or more of these things and it becomes camping. Sorry, can't do it. In the summer, when I'm barbequing, I don't even like walking onto the patio without shoes.

Why can't we just have a king-size bed, air conditioning, and a hot shower and call that camping? Well, we can't. That's called a trailer camper, and sorry, trailer campers are not camping. A trailer camper is a normal home, shrunk to discomfort size, put on wheels, and hidden among some trees.

But you know what it really is about camping? The animals. I don't like bears, beavers, raccoons, and birds and insects in my home. I don't think they really want me in theirs, either. And how can you feel good where you're not really wanted? A camper can. That's another reason that they are better people than me.

Curling Makes
Me Canadian

Recently, while I was travelling, a customs and immigration agent asked me my country of birth. I said, "Canada."

She said, "Do you have proof of citizenship?"

I said, "Yes, I watch curling."

"Thank you. Next!"

In my opinion, nothing makes me more Canadian than curling. Hockey, Mounties, maple syrup, back bacon, nothing (eh through zed) is more Canuck than curling. I was on the curling team in high school. Oh, sure, any dumb jock could play football. Any nerd could be on the chess team. But I curled, baby. I snapped those brooms, I pushed those brushes, I lifted those rocks until my body was granite. You yell "Hard, hard!" at me and I'm there for you, outside the house, in the house, out the back of the house. Curlers don't care where.

Well, those were my salad days. Now, I mostly watch curling on TV. I love instant replay. You can't watch a good "raise take out" enough times. And of course, the telestrator

— curling is such a fast-paced game, you need some guy with an electric pencil to explain what just happened. And you don't see the Nike swoosh on too many curling rocks. No, curling is above crass commercialism. Beer and cigarettes — those are the sponsors curlers hold out for.

You know, maybe we didn't invent the game, or some years even dominate, but curling is ours, man. Canada — a big sheet of ice with circles at either end. A bunch of men and women in sweaters going back and forth, sweeping. People say, "I love Canada, it's so clean." Well, that's why. We know how to sweep. Canada. The C is for curling.

Soccer As I See It

I find soccer a tough game to latch onto. I understand the basic aim, to get the ball into the big net, but after that, what's going on? The commentators assume if you're watching soccer, you already know exactly what the game's all about. I don't. So I've had to figure it out for myself from watching it on TV.

Here's what I've come up with. Soccer is played on grass, a huge expanse of lovely green grass about the size of Manitoba. Each team consists of about thirty players who all run willy-nilly about the field. Only one or two actually know where the ball is at any given moment. The rest must rely on updates from the newspaper, which is delivered daily to all players on the field. Each team has a goaltender, who refuses to wear team colours and in his own true spirit wears a lovely, stylish long-sleeve number with gloves, even if it's 105°C.

There are offsides in soccer, except that, once again, due to the size of the playing area, they can only be called from space with pictures from the Hubble telescope. By the time pictures are transmitted to NASA, then faxed to the playing field, the moment has often passed. There are referees who call penalties, which are in the form of cards. Yellow card, red card, sympathy card. The latter is the most serious. The game clock counts up, not down, and officials are allowed to add time to a game in the case of penalties. Or they can add time if they already paid for parking for the whole day anyway and they want their money's worth.

The average soccer game lasts three weeks. Soccer players run really fast and hard for the entire three weeks until the unlikely event that a goal is actually scored, then they run even faster and harder in an attempt to show enthusiasm and team spirit. All players play the entire three-week period. Substitutions are allowed only for weddings and funerals.

Soccer goals are few and far between. The record for most goals in a career belongs to Pelé, who played for over twenty years and still holds the record, six goals.

That's soccer. Understand that I've had to figure this out by myself without any help from the experts.

Hiking
Hiking

What is hiking, exactly? In an attempt to get and stay in shape I'm reading about various forms of exercise that go a long way toward helping you lead a healthy life. Walking, running, biking — those I understand. But they always mention hiking. What is hiking? As far as I can figure out, walking is part of hiking. However, if you are just out walking, you are not necessarily hiking. So when does the walking stop and the hiking begin? Well, that's the thing. I don't know. Say you're walking along a street, and you start to go up hill. Are you hiking? Possibly. But maybe the difference is distance.

"Can I walk to the train station from here?"

"Sure, but it's quite a hike."

I see pictures of people hiking among trees. Maybe that's it — you need trees. But trees could mean a stroll through the forest, not a hike in the woods. A stroll is very different than a hike. Sometimes you see photos of people hiking in the mountains. But isn't that really mountain climbing? Maybe hiking is just wimpy mountain climbing.

I do know that when you're hiking you need equipment. Walking shoes, running shoes — no, you need hiking boots. If you're wearing hiking boots and walking to the store, I can only assume you're hiking. Often, hikers have a big stick — a pole or a staff. And a backpack, and a big puffy vest. Now you're equipped for hiking, but how you actually hike is still a bit of a mystery to me. There are hiking trails. I've walked on them, and didn't particularly feel like I was hiking. We packed a lunch in our backpacks, I remember that. And that's good. Any exercise program where you stop halfway through to eat is fine with me.

Keeping the
Game Piece

Keeping the
Game Piece

As far as I know, hockey and baseball are the only sports where you are allowed to keep game pieces should they fly into the crowd during the course of a game. If a puck comes zinging at your head doing a hundred and fifty and you can grab it, it's yours, baby. Same with a baseball. Basketball and football, not so much. I guess the NBA and NFL are quite cash strapped so they really can't afford for you to have any free souvenirs. In the NFL they go to great lengths to ensure that one of their footballs is not kicked into the crowd. They string up a big net for the point after. It's lowered and raised as need be. Without the net, how many footballs do you think they'd lose in a game? Eight, on average. You figure the cost of the nets at either end, the framework to raise and lower them, the cost of the staff to operate them — wouldn't it be cheaper to just let the crowd have a few footballs?

Golf is different. If a ball goes into the crowd it's still in play. You can't have it. Golf is the only sport where spectators are allowed onto the playing field during the course of a game and the athletes must work around them. That would be interesting in hockey.

I just think all sports should have a blanket rule. If any game piece flies into the crowd during the event, the paying spectator should be allowed to keep it. This would be especially interesting in auto racing, and rodeo, if you think about it, and curling. Hopefully that'll never be an issue.

Free Admission
to All Sports

There should be free admission to professional sporting events according to the law, and I can prove it. Right now, if you want to go a professional sporting event, how much is it per ticket? $30? $50? $100? And if you actually want to go with someone, you can't afford it.

Now, how much do they charge you to go watch a taping of a television show, a game show, for example? Nothing. Why? Because they can't, they're not allowed. Television air waves belong to the public, and it's illegal to make money from a studio audience in the process of making your show. Oh sure, once the show is done, sell it to the networks, sell advertising, do what you want, but you can't charge people to become part of the studio audience.

I think you see where I'm going. Professional sports is nothing more today than a television show. The people in the crowd, nothing more than a studio audience to create the right atmosphere for me, watching from the comfort of my own home. Therefore, charging me $80 to become part of that studio audience is illegal. Sports is television,

television is sports — you can't argue with that. Replays, expert commentary, features, and highlights have made most pro sports much more enjoyable on TV than in person, where you're crowded into a hard plastic seat, there are loud drunks everywhere, you have to fight traffic, etc. Go ahead, charge me $5 for a hot dog once I'm there, $3 for coffee, $6 for a beer, I don't care. I'm there for free, according to the law. And believe me, they need a studio audience. Try watching a game when no one's in the crowd. It's boring. Just stop charging me, it's against the law. I think we have a case.

The Flood

I'm a hockey dad, a veteran hockey dad. And as a veteran hockey dad I may have to retire soon or be traded to another family. But over my years of going to hockey arenas, there is nothing quite as religious as the flooding of the ice. The "flood," we call it. Oh, a flood? We're on next, the flood's almost done. Can't wait. There's a flood, then we play. Oh yes, the flood.

If you've ever been a hockey parent, you know that hockey involves a lot of waiting. Oh sure, there are things to do — choose from the menu of fine cuisine and dine on the very best of rink food. Solve the problems of the world with the other hockey parents, get purple Thrills from the vending machine and make a big wad of gum. But you still have to wait your turn. Suddenly the game before you is over, and what happens? The flood.

As hockey dads, we gather at the altar of the arena and attend the flood. We are mere laymen compared to the Zamboni driver, but as veterans we know a good flood from a bad flood. A good Zamboni from a bad Zamboni, a good driver from a bad one. Oh sure, Mr. Rink-Maintenance Man, your stands are clean as a whistle, your vending machines flow freely with purple gum, but can you do a good flood? Twice around the circumference, then down the middle, then an oval pattern without fishtailing or spinning out, leaving no square inch of ice unflooded and ending perfectly at the Zamboni exit. That's a fine flood.

The ice is clean, fresh. It's like rebirth. *Let the game begin, there has been a flood.* I wish life were like that. Every time we had a bad day or a hectic week, life's little Zamboni would come by and give us a flood, and we'd be shiny and clean and ready for a new game. And boy, this just proves we do have too much time on our hands before a game. Either that or I've chewed too many Thrills.

The Duel

I think it's about time for the duel to make a come-back. It just seems like a nice, honourable way to settle things between two people.

"What do you mean you won't give me the bank loan? Take that!" A little glove across the face, you agree to meet at dawn, winner gets the honour — and the money. The duel just seems a lot simpler and more to the point.

But Larry, you're saying, isn't this promoting violence and guns? Well no, because in the classic duels, you chose your own weapons. In the old days it may have been pistols at ten paces, sabres to the death, but this is almost the 21st century. The new duels would choose weapons like Scrabble. The new duels would have gladiators battle in such titan competitions as remote-control channel-switching at ten paces, or who can crack their gum the loudest. It doesn't matter, as long as the duelers agree on the weapon and the competition. For one thing, this would end all frivolous lawsuits, not to mention all job-related disputes.

"Sorry, boss, what? I'm not getting the raise or the promotion?" Whip out the glove and give them one across the face. "Meet me at dawn, and bring those Scrabble tiles. I'm going to be merciless."

I think for day-to-day disputes, the duel wouldn't even be necessary. The glove-across-the-face part would give me enough satisfaction right there.

Food: It Helps Us Live

Junk Food

J unk food. I love it. It's good. Any food that you can comfortably consume in front of your TV, or in your car, or while wearing sweat pants falls into this category. If they had junk food restaurants, there would be a sign on the door that reads, "Sweat Pants Required."

If you're an aficionado like me, you know that junk food brings with it certain pleasures that only junk food can. I'm not talking about that fuzzy buzz you get in your head from the combination of sugar, chemicals, preservatives, and additives. I mean the simpler pleasures.

Nothing is more pleasing that having the big bag of Ruffles end at the same time as your tub of cream cheese onion dip. Often you have either chips or dip left over. In those cases, you have to either scoop the remaining dip out with your index finger and then quickly eat a chip or two, or, you must put the chip crumbs into the dip tub and eat them with a spoon, like you would cereal. But when both end at the same time, it's like the planets and the moon and the stars have aligned. Life is good.

There are so many other junk food pleasures, like when you eat your box of Smarties by colour and you discover you have bonus red ones. Or when eating a whole bag of pistachios you find the ones with no shells at the bottom. It's like a little reward for all the hard shelling you've done so far. The bag is saying, "Here's a few shelled ones, thanks for choosing pistachios. These last ones are on me, pal."

Nothing beats pulling a hard Snickers bar out of the freezer. Or how about when that Snickers has leaked and some of the creamy toffee nougat has welded itself to the wrapper? You eat the bar, but as a bonus, you get to suck the extra filling off the paper.

Even burgers and fries are a pleasure. (In my opinion, burgers and fries are on the border between junk food and a hearty meal.) There are always those bonus fries at the bottom of the bag. Spillage. Some people eat them as an appetizer before the entree. I personally like to save them for dessert.

But overall, you see what I'm really saying. Junk food has a euphoria all its own. Or maybe it's just the chemicals talking.

The Cereal Aisle

The Cereal Aisle

You probably already know this, but if you're going to take your kid down the cereal aisle of the grocery store, you don't stand a chance. If you were thinking that your child would be raised on "whole wheat no-sugar goodness" with granola and oatmeal as a treat, then you never realized you were up against Cap'n Crunch. Oh, you may be commander of the mother ship, but he is Captain of the entire cereal fleet. If the crunch wasn't enough to send your kid around the bend, there's always Froot Loops, Frosted Flakes, Corn Pops, Alpha Bits, and Cheerios. They're all your child's best friends — Fruity Pebbles, Count Chocula, Frankenberry. Hey, how's Trix? Or Cinnamon Toast Crunch, or Lucky Charms — they're magically delicious.

What chance do you, as an adult, have when the cereals you want to buy have names like Shredded Wheat, Bran Flakes, or Raisin Bran? None, really. Face it, your kid will never eat Muslix. For one, it's called Muslix. It's got an "x" in it and you don't even pronounce it. Basically, unless it's honey nut, apple cinnamon, frosted, or has marshmallowy goodness, your kid won't eat it. Even the good old basics like Corn Flakes and Rice Krispies come in flavours now. What is it with Rice Krispies? Some sweet old lady a long time ago invented tasty sweet squares out of this cereal, and now they've invented a cereal based on her squares. Rice Krispie Treats cereal, not to be confused with Rice Krispies with Marshmallows, a different part of this nutritious breakfast.

The other half of this is that we adults get ripped off. You see, they know how to name cereals with flavours and fun words kids will like — loops, bits, O's, crunch, cinnamon, chocolate, marshmallows. Adults should have cereals based on what we like for breakfast. "New from Kellogg's, it's Cold Pizza O's, Black Coffee and Donut Loops. From Post, it's Ham 'n' Egg Crunches, Cap'n Coffee 'n' Smokes." You know, those grown-up breakfasts. Instead of Snap, Crackle, and Pop, our little cartoon heroes would be Cough, Wheeze, and Spit.

Bread

I have a problem with bread. Yes, bread, the staff of life. The number one problem with bread is that, where I shop, it's in the first aisle of the store. You can't put it in the cart or it will end up at the bottom of your groceries. Okay zippy, you're saying, go to the last aisle and work back. Well, you can't. Fruit and vegetables are in the last aisle, and they really can't go at the bottom either. Canned and boxed goods are all in the middle aisles of the store, so I must start in the middle and work my way out in concentric circles.

But back to bread. Let's say the bread is in the last aisle, so the bread ends up on top. Then you go to the check-out line. The bread goes first onto the conveyor belt. You must be careful not to squash the bread with canned and boxed goods, which are now at the bottom but will be on top. You must trust the cashier to do the same, and watch her like a hawk. You see what I'm dealing with here. It's a big problem. Bread can't end up at the bottom. You've spent too much time and effort making sure it's on top. Okay, if the conveyor belt and cashier both do their job, the bread is safe. Now, you must reload the groceries bags into the cart, once again making sure that the bread ends up on top. Carefully peek into each bag to make sure the bread bags are all together and the cashier didn't hide a loaf of bread under anything else. Done. Bread is on top once again.

Now, I'm sure you see what the next task is. You must reload the groceries into the trunk of the car. What's first? Well, the bread's on top. The bread will end up at the bottom again if I'm not careful. The trick is to unload the entire top layer of groceries from the cart and place them strategically on the ground in the parking lot without having oranges roll down the pavement or any such dumb luck. Take the bottom layer of canned and boxed goods and load them in the trunk. Place the bread on the top trunk layer.

It's exhausting! I've tried giving the bread its own seat in the back, but the seat belt usually squashes it, or invariably one of the kids will sit on it. Or, after all that, you get it home safe and puffy and you bring it into the house and somebody sets it under the canned peaches in heavy syrup.

Basically, that's my problem with bread. I've never really solved it, except when I put each loaf into its own separate metal tackle box, but that got a little clumsy at the grocery store. The other thing I've learned to do is to enjoy flat sandwiches and toast.

The
Popsicle

The
Popsicle

Here's to the popsicle. I love you, popsicle. There aren't many treats you can still buy today with spare change. You're a little tight between paydays, it's hot, you can still get yourself a popsicle. When I was a kid, our store sold them really, really frozen. I always had to get my older cousin Randy to break them over the edge of the counter for me. Either that or eat them as a double-sticker. But then, one stick would eventually come out and you'd have a big hanging piece and it would fall in the dirt and you'd have to lick off the dirt, spit it out, and repeat until the popsicle was clean again.

Grape popsicles left the best drip stain on your shirt. Orange popsicles were the classic, and green was delicious. I guess green was lime flavour, but if anyone ever asked you what flavour it was, you just said, "green." Same with red. Red was my favourite flavour. When I was six, this girl Joanne used to rub red popsicle on her lips until it looked like she had lipstick on. Cool. Joanne became known as the small-town popsicle flirt. They had white popsicles for a while there when I was a kid. I don't know what they were, but they tasted like frozen 7UP.

What's the deal with chocolate popsicles? They were good, but really, why not just get a fudgsicle? True popsicle gourmands stayed with the fruit flavours. Grape, orange, red, and green.

Philip's mom used to make her own in an ice cube tray out of Kool-Aid or Jell-O powder. Nice try, Mrs. Phil, but those aren't popsicles, okay?

There aren't enough things in the world that make you feel like a kid again, but I'll tell ya, during the summer, a popsicle a day almost does it. And it's always fun around the office to try and explain how the grape stain got on your shirt.

Free Samples

Over the weekend, while I was grocery shopping, there were nine, count them, nine different little end-of-aisle kiosks cooking up free food samples. There was this new kind of Chinese food, a new kind of sausage, a new cracker, a new cheese (served on an old kind of cracker), some new shape of salty snack thing, a cake-ice cream deal, a new fruit cup, a new fruity beverage, and one more that I think was actually a new frying pan, so they were making all kinds of food.

Heck, who needs to buy food anymore? "Hi, table for two please, non-smoking, and I'd like to see a wine list. Oh, and it's her birthday, so if the cashiers could sing 'Happy Birthday' during our meal?"

Oh, and what a meal it was. Once I realized where all these freebies were located, I cruised around the aisles in order. I started with a few snacks and a fruity beverage aperitif, then moved on to some cheese and crackers, then sausages and Chinese food, finishing off with ice cream and cake and a fruit cup. And that's why I'm recommending this grocery store restaurant to all my friends.

Now, here's the etiquette. When you see this kindly older lady dishing out the freebies, you walk over and seem genuinely interested in the product (this is key). "Oh, are these those new crackers I've seen advertised on TV? I've always wanted to try one. I hear they're good." Basically, even though you're just there for the free snack, this makes them feel better and it gives them a better report to take back to head office. Now, 90 percent of the time you'll want to spit out the crap they give you, but don't. Always nod and use words like, "Mmmmm, interesting, different, unique, interplanetary." Next, always accept the coupon good for 30 percent off the product. Leave them with the illusion that you're actually going to take home this weird new food item. If they also have the product right there, accept that too. Then, just leave it behind the cereal or with the lettuce or someplace like that. Somebody will come and put it back eventually. Oh, if you actually like the food, seven minutes is a good rule: seven minutes of circling the store before you come back and get seconds. In seven minutes they usually forget you were there. Oh, and your kids, they get all they can eat. They love that. And I love it when they have free sample kiosks in grocery stores, because then I don't have to fill up at that other free sample place *they* choose to call the "bulk food section."

Cake for Breakfast

Do you like cake for breakfast? No. But millions of people throughout the world eat cake for breakfast every day. We all do it. You've done it. We call this cake "muffins."

It's time to stop kidding ourselves. Muffins are cake. Cake are muffins. Cake for breakfast? "Oh, no, no thanks. What, are you kidding? Cake! For breakfast? Never. A muffin? Why, yes please. Have you got carrot, or chocolate chip?" See, these are both names of cakes, but you think you're having a muffin.

Let's list some of the other so-called muffins and see how they stack up against cake. Blueberry? White cake with fruit that's rarely in season, yet somehow seems to be in muffins (I mean cake) year round. Cranberry? Same cake, different berry. Orange? Same cake, no fruit at all usually, just orange flavour. A corn muffin? That's easy. Corn cakes. Bran muffin? Really bad cake.

Then we get into a series of banana walnut, pecan oatmeal, etc. Those are from the series of loafs and breads, as in "banana bread," but really, banana bread is what? Cake!

Sure, no bacon, no sausages, no eggs for breakfast. My body is a temple. Just a coffee and a muffin please. You're having cake. Wake up. It's cake!

You know, the opposite is also true. You have a late dinner, good food, wine, you've got just enough room at the end for a little dessert. A muffin? "Oh, no, a muffin, are you kidding? For dessert? Haven't you got any cake?" See, once again. Muffins are cake, cakes are muffins.

Sometimes they fill muffins with fruit chunks and berries. Is that still cake? Well, now I think you're bordering on pie. Either way, except for the name "muffin," you're eating dessert as a breakfast food. You're eating cake. Why don't you just put a cup of Pepsi in the microwave to wash it down with? Hot Pepsi and cake. No, just a muffin and coffee, please, because after all, my body *is* a temple.

The Parental
Diet Book

The Parental
Diet Book

I'm thinking of writing a diet book. *The Parental Diet Book: How to Eat When You're a Mom or Dad.*

Chapter One: Baby Food. If baby doesn't want to eat strained peas, you are allowed to eat a teensy tiny bit and pretend to like it. If baby does not eat strained peaches, you are allowed to finish the entire jar. Strained-fruit baby food is delicious. I always thought, when I'm ninety and I have to eat this stuff once again, I'll have a pretty good time.

Chapter Two: Toddler Food. You are allowed to eat anything off the toddler's plate that they don't finish, as long as the food is recognizable. If a chicken finger still looks like a chicken finger, it's fair game after the toddler has gone out to play. If the chicken finger is indistinguishable from the potatoes or green beans, it's out, unless you really, really like chicken fingers. If part of the chicken finger is recognizable you may amputate it from its more disgusting half and eat it. This is how parents eat. This is how they must eat.

Chapter Three: Perishable Food. A parent must set an example and eat all food that may go bad. Fruit, bread, and leftovers are included. If the kids don't eat the bananas, and they're going brown, you must consume all eight bananas in one sitting, because otherwise it's like throwing away money. Chapter Three, subsection one: No matter how much a child enjoys their meal, they will never, never take leftovers to school for lunch. You must eat them before they are furry — again to set a good example.

Chapter Four: Leftover Pizza. It's every family member for themselves. First one to the fridge gets leftover pizza, or any other leftover take-out food. You are not allowed, even as a parent, to keep leftover pizza in your room. (Children, of course, do.) But you are the adult, you must leave it in a central, neutral location (the fridge) to ensure fair play. For a few years you will be bigger, faster, and stronger than your kids. You will usually get the pizza.

There will be thirty or forty chapters in my book altogether, including "Kids' Doggie Bags from Restaurants" (they are for mom or dad, we just pretend they're for the kids), and "Buying Junk Food and Zippy Cereal That Kids Would Like, Then Eating It All Yourself." And doctors wonder why the average Canadian has a lousy diet.

We're parents, that's why.

Bottled Water

How many different kinds of bottled water do you think there are? Ten, twenty-five, fifty? I'll bet there are more than fifty kinds. From fountains deep in the heart of France, from a spring in the hinterlands of British Columbia, from a glacier high in Vermont, blah, blah, blah. Name a province, name a country. They all have some secret underground supply of the best tasting, purest water in the world. Out of nowhere.

How many of you believe that some guy with a printing press made up some fancy labels and is standing there holding plastic bottles under the tap? Others say, how could that be? The bottled water people have to meet such strict standards. Yeah, three really high standards: quench my thirst, don't taste like Pennzoil, and don't kill me.

I guess some bottled water does taste better, and tests show that it is better, in *some* cases. What I want to know is, if there's all this mountain-fresh, glacier spring water by the shipload all over the world, why isn't it zipping out of the faucet every day? Why are we drinking the dishwater from the nearby river while the Baron de Perrier is buying villas and Ferraris with the money we spend on his H_2O?

Next thing you know, they'll be saying go ahead, breathe all the air you want. What's that? Oh, you want the *good* air. I'm sorry, that's $1.50 per bottle. Would you like the fresh air from deep in the heart of France, the hinterlands of B.C., or the glacier air from Vermont?

You know all this bottled water looks good and tastes good, but something is starting to smell funny.

The Cereal Box

The Cereal Box

When I was a kid, life revolved around the cereal box. That simple box of sugar-coated goodness provided me with education, recreation, and nutrition. What else do you need? Nutrition, sure, that's obvious. Every cereal is part of this nutritious breakfast, and provides 100 percent of the government's recommended daily intake of tiny marshmallows.

Education? Well, what kid hasn't sat semi-catatonic at the breakfast table shovelling in the puffs and krispies while reading the cereal box? I could read the same cereal box day in and day out for weeks. If Kellogg's knew that, they would've put homework on the cereal box and I might have passed geometry. As it was, the cereal box taught me French. As an Anglophone it gave me great bilingual skills, teaching me words like gratis, sucre, and riboflavin. Riboflavin, as a matter of fact, is the same in both languages. How's that for unity? My Canada includes riboflavin.

And recreation. Let me tell you. When I was a kid, there were great prizes at the bottom of the box. In one box

I actually found a bike. And never mind hockey cards. When I was a kid, actual NHL players were at the bottom of the cereal box. They would wait there until you finished the box, then sign an autograph (for free) and then go on to win the Stanley Cup. Oh yeah, those were the days.

When the box was finished, you could follow the directions and cut it up and make a telescope. That's how Hubble got started.

The cereal box ruled, man. Today, not so much. At least not for a grown up. After tasting the cereal, you might as well cut up the box and eat that. It provides 100 percent of the government's recommended daily intake of cardboardy goodness. Gratis.

I Love
Christmas,
I Really

Do

Getting the House Ready

There are several steps involved in getting the house ready for Christmas company.

The first step is cleaning and tidying. This will be done several times before the day of joy. Cleaning and tidying is what you do before company comes over so that they believe you live like this all the time. Of course, you don't. Would it be so bad for company to visit you when your house is like it usually is? "Hi, welcome to my Christmas party. Move those newspapers over and sit down. Throw your coat on the unmade bed, rinse out a glass, and pour yourself a drink." Wouldn't people feel more at home? Maybe not.

The next step — this is a tough one. Ask yourself: did any of the people coming to your home for the holidays buy you a gift last Christmas that should be on display? Keeping a master list on the computer is helpful. "Hi, Bob, Janet, come on in. You remember the cheese knife you bought us. Yes, it *is* always kept in its own stand beside the TV." Now, in case you miss one and someone asks, "Hey, where's that thing we bought you?" a kind response is always, "Oh, I don't have it anymore, but it did fetch the highest price at my garage sale." It makes them feel better.

The third step is decorating. Oh sure, the biggies are the Christmas lights, the wreath, and the tree. But now, in some Martha Stewart–induced frenzy, you must have everything related to Christmas. Candles, garland, Christmas candles, Christmas towels, dishes, tablecloths, and glassware. Okay, I give in. But I'm drawing the line at Christmas toilet paper. Yes, it's decorative, but there's just something unholy about it, even if it is just the reindeer. "Hey, Rudolph, thanks for coming. Sorry about the red nose." You know what? I think I'm almost ready for Christmas. Put the cheese knife by the TV and let the party begin!

Booking the Christmas Party

Booking the Christmas Party

We complain that the Christmas season starts earlier every year. Christmas cards are already in stores, Christmas lights and decorations are already sneaking into the displays everywhere, etc. But you know what's even worse? The staff Christmas party. It's becoming a twelve-month operation, and I pity you if you're the one in charge of it.

First of all, you have to book the venue for the staff Christmas party just before last call at last year's Christmas party, or chances are that this year you'll be at the drive-thru with the staff in a school bus asking if cranberry sauce is a condiment. You have to send out invitations because nobody reads memos anymore, and of course you have to chase half the staff around for the RSVP. Women are already worried about what they're going to wear, men are already worried that if there's a game on that night, then where can they watch it? (I hate to generalize, but come on, it's true!) When both people in a couple work, each complains about being dragged to the other's stupid party. And don't forget to book a babysitter or you'll end up with fourteen-year-old

Elvira, the Queen of the Dark from two doors down who just pierced her entire head. Lately, some workplaces are giving themes to their staff Christmas parties. They try to come up with some clever theme idea. Hey, here's a good theme: Christmas.

Once you're there, you see the same spouses from last year whose names you've already forgotten. The food is questionable. Last year, in a classic turnabout, my boss got drunk and said what *she* really thought of *me*.

Why is it again we do this? Oh yeah, it's Christmas.

Merry Christmas
to All

Has this ever happened to you? You're in a store or somewhere at Christmas, you're about to leave and the clerk says, "Merry Christmas."

You say, "You, too," then walk outside and think, "Gee, I'm not sure, in this rich ethnic mix we call Canada, if that person celebrates Christmas. Maybe I just insulted them."

If you think you've done this, do what I do. March right back in and say, "Look, I just inadvertently wished you a Merry Christmas and frankly I'm not sure if that was the right thing to do according to your particular religious beliefs, because frankly I don't know that much about other religions. It's not that I don't want to know, it's just I haven't had the time, what with the house and kids and work and all. What I meant to say was "Merry 'Whatever' and Happy 'Ya Know,'" unless of course your holiday is not supposed to be happy. That's providing you are having a holiday sometime in the next little while. So good luck, if you even believe in luck, with whatever you're doing within your own faith over the next few weeks. Fasting in the month of

January during daylight, or conducting a series of services with candles, according to some sort of book and/or religious icon. If dancing is involved, I hope that goes well. Singing or praying in any manner facing a certain direction in a gathering of like-minded people in a solemn or happy way on a specific or non-specific day of the week in a special kind of building . . . and just . . . well . . . I think I speak from the heart when I say . . . have a nice day."

They usually respond with, "You too."

On the
Road
with

Larry F.

The First
Bike

The First
Bike

Remember your first bike? Me neither. But I do remember my daughter's first bike. Later, it became my son's first bike, and boy, was he pleased about that. But you know, pink can be a good colour for a boy. This time of year, when I pull my old bike out of the garage and go for that first ride, I can, for a brief moment, remember my first bike. Maybe not that same bike exactly, but I remember the glorious feeling of learning to ride a two-wheeler, the feeling of freedom when the training wheels come off and dad lets go and you're on your own. The exhilaration of the speed, the confidence, the power, the pain that comes with landing in the neighbor's hedge — oh, it all rushes back.

The actual bike I don't recall that well. I do recall perfectly going to pick out my daughter's first two-wheeler: pink, white tires, a white basket with daisies on it (the same kind of daisies that prevent slippage in the tub), fluorescent pink streamers. We added those little pink and orange balls on the spokes. You can see how it was that when my son inherited the bike he was a big hit with all the other boys in the neighbourhood.

We also added this six-foot bright orange flag on the back so that my daughter could be seen between parked cars and from down the street and so she could poke dad in the eye every time she put the bike down. You'd think that since the flag was bright orange I would see it coming. But no, time after time I'd stand on the wrong side. "Ow, flag in the eye, flag in the eye. Don't cry, dear, daddy's fine. Now, go get mommy to call the ambulance."

I still see kids out there every day on new little two-wheelers with flags wearing bike helmets, learning to ride from moms and dads and brothers and sisters. I don't want to get preachy, but when you see them, don't be in a hurry. Slow down, give them their time and their space, and enjoy the moment, because it's over so quickly.

Recently I had to teach my daughter how to drive a car. Where did the time go? Thinking back to teaching her how to ride a bike I asked myself, "How do I do this again?" Well, I held onto the back of the minivan until she was going pretty good, then I let go without her knowing, and sure enough, she was driving on her own.

Minivans Are
Still Vans

Minivans Are
Still Vans

D on't you think it's about time we took the word "mini" out of "minivan"? Face it — you're driving a van. Yeah, there may be vans bigger than yours, but you are still driving a van. Just because years ago Lee Iacocca got the idea to call it a minivan is no reason to continue to use the term. In the last five years they've even come out with "extended" minivans, and extra-added minivans. You see what they're doing. They're taking a van, making it smaller, then making it bigger, the whole time still calling it a minivan.

You're driving a *van*. I know. I drove one for four years. I thought I had a big car. It drove like a car. The ads even said, "Drives like a car." *Like* a car, not *is* a car. I was driving a van.

"We're all going up to the lake this weekend. Larry will drive, he's got a van." All of a sudden I was the unofficial president of the hockey team car pool. "Larry, can you take the kids to practice? You've got that van."

"Hey, you know what? Why don't I just install a little dinger that you can pull when it's your stop?" There was always something.

"Larry, we're moving this weekend. Can we borrow your van?"

Mini shmini. If I was driving a Geo or a Miata, nobody would be bugging me to help deliver four sheets of drywall when they're working on their basement. Also, you feel guilty in rush hour traffic driving all alone. People stare at you as if to say, "Look at that guy, all by himself in a huge van."

You see, Geo or Miata — that's "mini." A van is a van is a van. Stop kidding yourself.

Is That My Old Car?

Have you ever done this? I do this all the time. I'm driving down the street and I see a car that looks *exactly* like a car I used to have. And I think, *maybe that is the car that I used to have.* I always try and get close to it, to see if I'll recognize it for sure. Does it still have that little freckle over the left fender? Are those the seatbelts that used to caress me, now around the arms of someone new?

If I get a chance, I'll ask the driver, "How do you like her?" I hate it when they try and speed away. I hate it when they don't answer. I hate having to chase them. I hate it when the police come.

I thought I saw my old white minivan the other day. Oh, I know there were at least a thousand like her, but I think this was really her. Oh yes, it was a "her," though I don't know why. It just was. I'm not a typical guy in that sense, though. I don't call all of my cars "her," or "she." I used to have a Chevy that was definitely a he. Once I had this Euro sports car that was more of a hermaphrodite. No, wait, that was only the name of the car — a brand new 1978 2-door Hermaphrodite. It looked like a Fiat.

There are a couple of cars, like that one, where if I thought I saw it on the street I would just pull up my collar, turn my head, and walk by really fast, hoping it wouldn't recognize me. But when I think I see the others, like the old white minivan, I say, "Hey, look at that one. I think that one was mine." We just grew apart you know, the time had come. So now she's with someone else. If you have a white minivan, it might have once been mine, so please take good care of my baby.

A Guy with the Same Car

I recently moved into a new neighbourhood. In the 'hood, there's a guy who has exactly the same car as me. One of us is going to have to move.

I knew when I bought my car that they had probably built ten thousand cars just like it — the same year, model, colour, wheel covers, interior, etc. But I didn't think there would be one *down the street*. I know you think it should be me because I'm new to the neighbourhood, but just maybe I got my car before he did, so he should have to move, or he should have to get another car.

Furthermore, manufacturers must have a computer base of car owners and where they live. They should simply not allow two of the exact same cars within a ten- or maybe even a twenty-block radius. There should be some kind of system — if you're looking for a new neighbourhood, you first have to contact your car dealer so they can tell you where the cars exactly like yours are located, and where you could move so you would have the only car like it in the area.

When you buy a new car, you'd first have to give them your address. They would check their computer, and could say, "Sorry, we can't sell you a black two-door. There's one exactly like it two streets over." This would avoid the embarrassment of having exactly the same car as someone else in the neighborhood.

And if something did sneak through the car dealer computer system, your real estate agent's computer should have a back-up system. "This is a lovely house, in your price range, perfect for you, but sorry, they already have a green Tempo next door. I can't accept your offer." To me, this is what the computer age is all about.

Money:
The Root
of Some

Nutshells

How To Pay Bills

How To Pay Bills

I hate paying bills. I despise it. I loathe it. If I made a list of my least favourite things to do, five feet beneath where I buried the box with the list in it would be paying bills. Who really likes to pay bills? No one.

My bank does provide a phone service I can use to pay my bills with a simple touch-tone phone. I don't use it. It's not a matter of trusting the system, which I don't. I just can't seem to be bothered to learn it. Every few months I call the bank, and they send me the brochure and my secret access code and I shove it in with the bill pile and say to myself, "Okay, next month, for sure." Then I get lazy and don't do it. Of course, I could just walk into the bank and take up valuable teller time and pay the bills all in one shot, but for some reason I just don't. For one thing, there's always a line-up, and not only that, everybody in front of me always looks like they're packin' and about to commit a felony. Then I'd have to lie down on the floor, stay still, not breathe, wait for the police, give a statement

— that's all providing I wasn't taken as a hostage in the first place. Boy, that would put a dent in my week.

So I pay my bills the old-fashioned way, which is probably why I hate bill paying. Once a month I sit at my desk with the cheque book and decide who gets the money. And this is how I try to make it fun for myself. I take ten bills, put them in a box, shake it around, and then pick the five places that will get my money this month. I'll pay the next five next month, or whenever they get picked in the pay-your-bills lottery. There's another way I try to make it more fun. If any bill is over $100, I write "Attention: Bloodsuckers" on the envelope. This way I get a big laugh out of it, and I'm sure it makes them chuckle down at the bloodsucker office.

You know who has the best idea — people who *never* pay their bills. That way, people actually show up at their house to collect the money. No fuss, no muss. No access codes, no bank tellers, no cheques, no stamps, no nothing. You want my money, you come and get it.

Expensive Watches

I don't understand why people want to have an expensive watch. Down the street at my local House of Crud (also known as the Dollar Store) I can get watches for around $2 or $3 apiece. So what if those watches last only a couple of months? I can always get another one. For $20 I could go for a couple of years and always have the correct time. Why would I buy an expensive watch?

It could be because cheap watches look cheap. At the department store, I can buy a nice designer watch for $30. Well, maybe not made by a famous designer, but it looks nice, and has a leather strap and a three-year warranty.

But people pay several hundred dollars for a watch, or even several thousand. And you know, frankly, I can't tell the difference. Besides, my $29.95 watch does have that three-year warranty. For $39.95 I can also get a chronograph, a stopwatch, and I learn the phases of the moon, a very important aspect of timekeeping. You know how it is. You promise your date you'll be there by quarter moon and you show up half-past full moon, or full-past half moon. You're late, and you're putting strain on your relationship.

Expensive clothes are often nicer than cheap clothes, an expensive car seems more luxurious than a cheap car, and sometimes expensive food is better than cheap food. But expensive watches — I just don't get it. I don't work for NASA or set any atomic world clock. What's it worth to me to know the time? About $29.95. If you'd like to discuss this topic further at any time, meet me at the House of Crud at 2:00 p.m., or 2:05, or 2:10, or quarter moon. Sometime around then.

A Bank
for Kids

A Bank
for Kids

What we need is a kids' bank. A bank for kids, about kids, run by kids. As a parent you're saying, "Hey, *I'm* my kids' bank." Exactly. That's exactly why we need one. As early as possible, kids should have to deal with the realities of banks, credit, and getting into debt for the rest of their lives.

It would do a kid good, even at the age of eight, to go into Kids' Bank and wait in line to make an appointment with the loan officer.

"Mr. Johnson, I'd like to take out a second mortgage on my Nikes. I need some new laces. They need a cleaning, and I really would like to do some shoe improvements. Income? Well, I deliver the local paper and I get $5 for mowing the lawn and shovelling the walk. My kiddie Visa balance is really low and I only have one other outstanding loan — I owe my older brother $7.50. I'm willing to offer some pizza coupons and a 49ers' hat as collateral."

Kids would have cheque books and bank cards. All the employees would be kids so there would be more jobs out there for them. Only kids would be allowed as customers.

"Dad, wait in the car and don't play around with the radio. I won't be long. Geez, look at the line-up."

I'm sure eventually you'd have kiddie bank robbers, so you'd have to have kiddie police, but let's deal with that when it happens. Kids could have credits, loans, debt, financial problems, three mortgages, and would worry, fret, lose their hair, and declare bankruptcy — all by the time they finish elementary school. Then they'd join the high-school bank and be ready for the real world within four years. Attention all parents: I'll be circulating a petition soon.

Men and Women

What Flowers Say

S ay it with flowers. But say what exactly? As a man, if you show up with any old bouquet of flowers, you're doing pretty good. Well, apparently not. According to this calendar I picked up at a florist, different flowers say different things. I guess I kind of knew this, but this calendar opened my eyes, and my nostrils, in a different way.

For example, giving roses is a good idea, if they're red, white, or pink. But a yellow rose can mean slighted love, according to this calendar. "Sorry dear, I just though yellow was your favourite colour. I didn't mean anything by it." I've also heard that a single yellow rose says, "Goodbye, it's been nice." It's very confusing.

Lilies are a lovely flower. White lilies represent purity and modesty, but yellow ones mean falsehood. What would half a dozen yellow lilies say to a loved one? "Here are some flowers. I'm lying. I don't mean it."

Apparently the snapdragon means presumption. The buttercup is childishness. A certain kind of carnation means refusal. You see what I mean? You're playing with a loaded weapon here. You just want to be nice and you're possibly telling someone they act like a kid, you're giving them the boot, or that they're presumptuous.

Never mind what you're saying with a dozen larkspurs, or phlox, monkshood, yarrow, periwinkle, or a venus flytrap. Well, I think we all know what we're saying with the flytrap. Giving flowers is way too complicated. On the next special occasion, I'll say it with cash.

Labelling
Washrooms

C ould we please pass some kind of law that states public washrooms must be labelled "MEN" and "WOMEN" in big block letters and no other way? You could have "men" and "women" in ten different languages if you wanted. You could maybe even add those little universal symbols, the stick man and the stick woman (the one in the skirt) to indicate gender, but that's it.

Bars and restaurants have taken the washroom sign thing to another dimension. You're in a bar, having a margarita and some nachos, when nature calls. You make your way downstairs to the washroom, finally find the hallway, only to have to stop and think, "Am I a cabellero or a señorita? Am I the matador, or the woman with the fan on her head? What's with the pictures on the doors? Which door is for me?" Of course you're saying, "Well, Larry, that's easy. You're a matador." You're probably right, but since when is going to the washroom supposed to be a test?

If we do have to be tested, the test should always be easy. In one bar I was in, one of the washrooms had a picture of a matador with a señorita in the background cheering him on. I guessed that this was the men's room, but is a woman supposed to come in and applaud me? In another place I was trying to figure out if the men's washroom had the picture of two women drinking tea near some flowers, or the one of a guy in a raft going over a waterfall. I guessed I was the guy on the raft, but this after a few cocktails . . .

MEN. WOMEN. Big signs, big block letters. Please. It's too bad the big "P" is used by parking lots. That would certainly help out, too.

Why Men Don't Ask for Directions

Why Men Don't Ask for Directions

Here's the reason men don't ask for directions: somebody may actually give us some. That's why. Simple, but true. Directions are almost always impossible to follow. Anybody's idea of how to get there and how long it takes differs from someone else's. Go ahead, ask some people how to get somewhere, and, for even more fun, ask when you should leave to get there on time.

Five different people will give you five different suggestions.

"Leave at four."

"No, earlier, you're fighting traffic."

"No, leave later. Just take the freeway."

"No, not the freeway. Use the sideroads."

"Sideroads? Are you nuts? They're under construction."

Never mind. I'll leave now, camp out, and keep on going tomorrow morning. Just tell me how to get there.

Everybody has their own little map in their head. According to this map, they know the fastest route to get to where you are going. People always tell you how many sets of lights to go through. It's never right. They either forget to count a set, or don't count the lights you actually turn at or the set of lights you start off from. As soon as someone says to you, "Go through three sets of lights," roll up your window and drive on.

People are also very good at telling you where *not* to go. "If you see a church you've gone too far. There's a big pine tree on the hill. You don't want that. The road up there goes left, but don't take it." Just tell me where I *can* go.

People also remember landmarks in their own way. The Shell station may actually be a Sunoco. The Coffee Time could be Bob's Donuts, or the bank might be a grocery store.

Street names are of no help. Someone will confuse Oak with Elm and Third Avenue with Third Street.

This is why men have it right. Don't bother asking for directions. Drive around hopelessly and eventually you'll get there. That's our motto. With directions you still drive around hopelessly and there's no guarantee you'll even get close.

In the old days they had it right too. Keep going that way, and when you fall off the edge of the earth, you've gone too far.

Too Much
Perfume

Too Much
Perfume

Somewhere, as we speak, someone you know or will come in contact with is putting on far too much perfume or cologne. The sense of smell is one of the most subtle yet powerful senses we have, but that doesn't matter to these people. They are filling their tubs with Oscar de la Renta. One guy has a turtle pool full of Brut beside his bed. In the morning he rolls over, falls in, gets dressed, and goes to work. The fragrance might have been mildly intoxicating, but now it's more like an obnoxious drunk — in your face, offensive, and irritating.

Every day we are forced to sit next to these people on the subway or bus, in the car pool or workplace. It's like walking by the Clinique, Lancôme, and Estée Lauder counters all at once. Men are no better than women. Putting on cologne is like spraying Pam on a non-stick surface: you just don't need that much.

It's not that much better once these people leave the room. These smelly people leave a vapour trail like a comet's tail. You can walk around and determine exactly where they've been by the aroma of Calvin Klein still lingering in the air. Your eyes water, you start to sneeze, and your coffee tastes funny. Someone says, "I guess Ken's in the building."

In ancient Rome they used perfumes and lotions instead of bathing. People — it's no longer ancient Rome. Arrivederci aroma. Just a hint of fragrance. Please.

Television: It's Catching On

Why Talk to the Contestants?

Why do they interview the contestants on game shows? They do it on *Wheel*, they do it on *Jeopardy*. They've done it on almost every game show I've ever watched since I was a kid. On *Jeopardy*, Alex Trebek interviewing his guests is sixty seconds of the most painful television you've ever watched. On *Wheel*, Pat Sajak is actually quite good at it. So good, in fact, that at one point they decided Pat should have a show without a game, where he just interviewed people full time. Turns out he wasn't that good, 'cause now he's back on *Wheel*.

Frankly, I don't want to know *anything* about these contestants on the game shows. I don't care what clubs they belong to, what they do back home, or that they once got a hole-in-one. It does not add to my enjoyment of the game show to know that Janice has two sisters who are both in the audience. They aren't famous, and this isn't *The Tonight Show*. Leno's guests are barely tolerable, so why would I want to spend valuable game show time learning about the interests of *Jeopardy* contestants? I just want to play the game at home.

One game show almost never asks. Bob Barker on *The Price Is Right* doesn't ask and doesn't care. "Welcome to the stage, Dave, here's our next prize . . . a new car! Here's the game: 'Bull's Eye.' You lose, Dave. Leave the stage. Come back for the Showcase Showdown." See, no questions about his personal life. *The Price Is Right* is the longest running, most successful game show of all time. I think that's why.

Home
Taping

I don't know exactly when it happened, but I now have more hours of TV recorded on video tapes than I could ever watch. These aren't feature films from that video club I joined in a weak moment. This isn't Ken Burns's *Baseball* or any other series not available in stores, available only for a limited time through this special TV offer. This is the dreaded "home taping."

Often I do watch the programs I tape. "Oh, Larry, that's a good episode of *The X-Files*, don't want to miss it, better tape it." The problem begins when you have to tape over something. "Gee, that season finale of *Seinfeld*, I don't want to tape over that. I'll probably want to watch it again some day." Sure you will.

"Hey guys, come on over Saturday, big party at my house. We're going to watch the season finale of *Seinfeld* from 1992." Truth is, I'll never watch it again, but I still save it. You have tapes of family events or movies you really like, but what do you do with all that other stuff you've taped and saved?

The final episode of *M*A*S*H*, that'll come in handy. The second Blue Jays' World Series win. Why tape a three-hour baseball game when all you want is the homer Joe Carter hit in the last thirty seconds of the game? Once I accidentally taped three hours of the weather channel. I still have it. Thought it might be neat to look back one day at the weather for November 9, 1993. Oh, and I taped *Late Night* that time Madonna was on. I'd better save it. You never know when I might want to watch Madonna mouth foul language again.

Do I put some sentimental value on these home tapings? No, not really. Do I think it might be worth something someday? No. Basically, I'm an idiot. Thousands of other idiots tape this junk every day and then refuse to tape over it. If they had had VCRs in 1969 and we had all taped the moon landing, do you think we'd ever watch it? No, of course not. I could tape the TV news every year on my birthday for thirty years, and thirty years later, who would want to see it? No one, not even me. Yet we save tapes and then hunt through the bargain bin at Zellers for new fresh video tapes to record more stuff that we'll never watch.

I'm going to stop. I vow to start taping over stuff . . . except the three hours of the weather channel. That might be worth something someday.

Make the Theatre More Like Home

Make the Theatre More Like Home

People spend a lot of money trying to make home theatre as close to the real thing as possible, buying big screens and speakers, just so that seeing a movie at home will be like seeing it in a theatre. What a waste of time.

For one thing, it's expensive and technology gets better so quickly that you have to keep upgrading your system. Here's a much better idea. They should attempt to make the movie house experience more like watching a tape at home.

Let me explain. You're sitting in the movie theatre and all of a sudden you hear, "Larry, phone! It's your mother."

"But they're about to capture that guy — "

"Pick up the phone, it's your mother."

Or, you're at the movies and you hear, "The dryer stopped. Check the towels to see if they're dry. I think they need ten more minutes."

Wouldn't it be great to be in the big theatre with Dolby THX and everything and be able to say, "Can you pause this? I gotta go to the bathroom, and I'm going to stop by the fridge on the way back, anybody want anything?"

Instead of popcorn, soft drinks, and candy, how about theatres have a big fridge full of stuff like leftover meatloaf, half a jar of pickles, and yesterday's macaroni salad? You could run back into the theatre and yell, "Honey, when is that lasagna from? Do you think it's still good?"

Never mind making home more like the movies. Make the movies more like home.

.

Larry F.'s One-Stop Shopping Section

Small Liquor Bottles

Small Liquor Bottles

I love the little liquor bottles they sell near the cash register at the liquor store. Usually in the retail world that's where they put the impulse buys — near the cash register. But is it good to buy small amounts of liquor on an impulse?

You're picking up a bottle of wine for dinner and you're waiting in line and you say to yourself, "Hey, maybe we should have a couple of shots of this mysterious blue liqueur." And nothing sits inside the jacket pocket at a concert better than a couple of little bottles of Drambuie. Going to the movies? Why not take three or four miniature bottles of Kahlúa in case Jean-Claude Van Damme gets boring?

I'm not sure who buys those little bottles of booze. I guess they're cute. As kids we thought they were cute. Little mini-versions of the stuff mom and dad were drinking. It's important, when going to the liquor store, to pick up a little something for the kids.

The only way you used to be able to get these miniatures was on an airplane. A friend of my dad's collected the little mini-bottles he got on airplanes. It was his own little travelogue of where he'd been. No souvenirs, no photographs, just lines and lines of little mini-liquor bottles. He could take you on a little tour of his excursions.

"Ah, here was a business trip to Chicago in '78. I drank four Canadian Clubs there and three Smirnoffs on the way back. These twelve Captain Morgan rum bottles are from when the wife and I went to Hawaii. And these three brandies were a little commuter flight to Edmonton."

Oh, the stories he had. Considering the number of little bottles he'd saved, it was more like the stories he'd forgotten. But his collection is no longer special because we can now buy all the miniature liquor bottles we want at the cash register of the liquor store. For my next party I'm going to buy only miniatures, then sit there and drink four bottles of vodka. The next day I'll complain about my little miniature hangover.

Picking Your Own Berries

I always see signs like this on country sideroads: "Pick Your Own Berries." I know what the farmer is really saying. "Hey, if you'd like to save some money, walk around my dirt, pick your own berries, give me a few cents for the actual fruit, and then be on your way. Please, come on in, pick your own berries." Sure, that's what it means *now*.

But is that how it started? I don't think so. Next time you're driving by a pick-your-own-berries farm, try reading their sign like this: "Pick your *own* berries." It's like when someone steals food off your tray. You say, "Hey, get your *own* French fries." I think it's the same attitude with these berry farms.

I'm sure a long, long time ago city people went for drives outside the city and pulled into farmers' yards and said, "Couldn't help notice your big berry patch. Wonder if we might have a few. Be glad to pay you for them."

"Sure," said the friendly farmer as he was working in the dell.

The city folk waited, and when the farmer kept working, they said, "Aren't you going to pick them for us?"

"Well, sure. Okay," obliged the friendly farmer because, as we know, farmers are friendly because, well, they're farmers.

You can see how the word spread that farmers were friendly, and that you could get baskets of fruit for jams, jellies, and healthy snacks for the cost of the berries alone.

After a few fruity seasons, farmers' other crops were in disarray, the farm animals were lethargic and skinny, and the barnyard was run down because the farmer was out picking berries for the city folk for free.

Finally, after trying to get some work done in the dell, one farmer finally snapped. He looked up at some friendly city slicker and said, "Hey, pick your *own* berries." In case this wasn't enough to get the word out, the farmer put a sign up by the road leading to his property. "Pick your *own* berries," which the city people, ignorant to the ways of rural life, read as "Pick your own berries."

Remember, when you see one of these signs, that first farmer, years ago, who finally snapped and put an end to the practice of picking your berries for you, just so he could get some work done in the dell.

Cashier School

There should be a cashier school. Maybe the local community college should offer a course in cashiering. Right now, when you get a job anywhere as a cashier, you learn how to work the machine, the scanner, etc., but you don't learn *how to be a cashier*.

For example, don't give me pennies unless you really have to. If the bill is $1.41 and I give you a toonie, give me sixty cents change. Not fifty-nine cents, but sixty cents. Eat the penny. Some cashiers do that and some don't. There's no industry standard.

Also, does the receipt from the cash register go in the bag or in your hand? I'll bet ninety percent of people want their receipt in the bag. The worst cashiers hand you the receipt, your folding money, and your coins all in a big pile in one hand. Now *you* have to separate the bills from the coins from the receipt. It's no good. That's *their* job.

What's the industry standard on saying "have a nice day"? Some cashiers say it, some don't. My feeling is, it should be dropped altogether. Really, it's my own business what kind of day I choose to have, and how can I have a nice day when you just gave me all the pennies in a big pile with my receipt, which I wanted in the bag? You've just ruined my day.

These are the things you could learn in cashier school. If cashiers did well in a six-week night-school course, they would get a diploma and it would be in the bag.

Fun at the Grocery Store

Fun at the Grocery Store

And now, fun you can have in the check-out line at the grocery store. Let's face it, it's kind of boring to watch the clerk scan your grocery items, so it's up to you to jazz it up a bit. Beat those grocery-buying blahs.

First, if buying spices, make sure you buy a bottle of ground thyme. It'll cost you over $4. When the cashier's ringing it up, say, "Wow, thyme really *is* money." It kills them every time.

Complain about the cost of each and every item you purchase. The 16-year-old high school student working weekends as a cashier loves to hear you complain. It leaves them with a good sense of what to look forward to when they're old enough to do their own grocery shopping.

If you're buying a newspaper at the grocery store, tell them you think some of the news has gone bad, so you only want to pay for the news you like. It won't work, but it sure is fun to watch them go *"huh!??!"*

When the check-out clerk is weighing all the fruit, say, "I know how much apples cost, but hey, Mr. Tally Man, tally me banana." If that gets a rise out of them, finish the song.

When they bag a really light item, say a loaf of bread, ask them to double bag it because you have to walk home. When buying a lot of groceries, ask if they can put each item in its own bag, and when they're done, ask them to double bag them.

This is my favourite: Fill a shopping cart to the brim, go through the check out, then when the cashier's about halfway through ringing in your items say, "Oh, sorry, this is the wrong peanut butter. Can I run and exchange it?" Then, sneak out of the store and go home. Loads of laughs, but remember, you can only do it once per store.

Shopping When Hungry

There's an old adage that says never go grocery shopping when you're hungry. I've never really understood this. I'm hungry, I need food, I have no food, what should I do? Should I sit around and wait until I'm full? Ain't going to happen. It's more fun to shop when you're hungry, because then you get something you want. Let's face it, the grocery store freezer has a better selection than your freezer at home, and their produce section is better stocked than your crisper. If you're at home and you crave chicken and you have none, what good is that? Shop when hungry, I say.

Have you ever gone to a grocery store right after dinner? No, no one does. No one sits at home and says, "Well, dear, let's strap on the old feedbag then go food shopping." Yet we constantly hear the saying "never shop when you're hungry, 'cause you'll buy stuff you don't need." Baloney. (Mmmm, baloney.) I think this is a myth promoted by fast-food places. Don't food shop hungry, chow down here first. That's how they screw you.

I already apply this principle to all other aspects of my life. I never go clothes shopping naked. I shop for a new car while I still have an old car. I don't wait till I'm homeless before finding a place to live.

But I like to food shop when I'm hungry. Men food shop hungry, and yet they always seem to find a new girlfriend when they already have a wife or girlfriend. We don't want to end up with something we didn't really want and have it turn out to be just a craving.

Chaining Carts Together

M any national grocery chains today are part of a cruel and inhumane practice: They chain grocery carts together. It's true. You've seen it, I've seen it. We may hate to admit it, but maybe we've even been a part of this torture. I know if *people* were chained together we'd be in an uproar. Seeing animals chained together would make us all weepy, yet every day, in parking lots across the nation, grocery carts are chained together and herded into little corrals.

Some are left out all night, others are herded indoors at random. Some end up with a pushed-in face, or a bum wheel. It's no wonder that sometimes, while you're loading your groceries into your trunk, a cart will try to roll away, to escape down the parking lot. Few of them make it. Sure, some find refuge in people's garages and on balconies, but how many times have you seen one wheels-up in the ditch, only blocks away from the corral? It didn't make it. It's sad. And what does it cost to free these prisoners? Only twenty-five cents per cart. But we don't free them. We use the carts for our own purposes, then we want our quarter back so we chain them back up.

One day I'm going to get a roll of quarters, maybe two, and go to the parking lot on a Sunday night and set them all free. I'll be like the grocery-cart Greenpeace. I'll slip a quarter into the slots, pop the chains, and shout, "Run away! Run away!" I'll sing "Born Free" at the top of my lungs. After that I'll only shop at grocery stores that have "free-range" carts. That's how I can make a difference.

Larry F. Sits Around the House

No Phones at Dinner

A round my house we had a rule: no phones during dinnertime. The rule lasted about eight minutes. My son's and daughter's friends were not aware of the rule, or perhaps do not eat dinner, and this is why they choose to phone at dinnertime. Dinner is usually around six. As soon as we sit down, the phone rings. However, we've sat down to eat as late as seven or seven-thirty and the phone rings. We've sat down to eat as early as five, and the phone rings. It doesn't matter when. They just seem to know when it's dinner. I think they're watching us.

Of course, the phone's never for me. Well, not *never*. Just the other day I got a call at dinnertime. "Dad, it's for you. Some guy wants to know if you want new windows and doors."

Yes, I'll take that call. "Hello, yes, I want new windows and doors, the kind that keep people from knowing when we're having dinner, so they don't phone us. Do you have those? Can you get them here now? Would you like to join us for dinner? Hope you don't mind cold food, which is what I'm having because I'm sitting here talking to you."

With the magic of the cordless phone, we can have all of the calls right *at* the dinner table. It's like having company every night.

I just gave up on the rule. Phone anytime. What's the use of a rule that nobody follows and that you can't enforce? As a matter of fact, I've gotten so used to it that if we don't get a call during the evening meal, I pick up the phone and start calling people. I always start with the windows-and-doors guy.

Toastercide

Toastercide

I'm tired of my toaster telling me which side I'm allowed to toast one slice of bread on. It's not right. If I want to make one cup of tea, my kettle doesn't tell me which side to boil the water on. But the toaster has some sort of attitude. One slice? Little arrow pointing, this side only. Do it my way.

I'm sure that when I put one slice of bread in the toaster, I see *both* sides light up. I'm positive that both elements are burning, so why does it choose sides? Why does *it* get to choose sides? Why isn't that *my* choice? Maybe I don't feel like making toast on the right side, the side with the arrow. Maybe I want to see what one slice of left-side toast tastes like. I can't. It's against the toaster rules. I don't think small appliances should have rules. Well, maybe one: Do not use the toaster in the bathtub. But that's it.

Sometimes when I only want one slice of toast, I'll purposely make two just so as not to give my toaster the satisfaction of running my life. It doesn't make sense that a toaster would have a "one slice — this side" rule. Over the course of several loaves, that one side would be overworked.

The right side is going, "Hey, I'm working when there's two slices, I'm working when there's one slice, when do I get a slice off?" You'd think the toaster workload would be more evenly distributed over time if you got to choose the one-slice side, but you're not the boss of your toaster, your toaster is the boss of you. One of these days, maybe at a Christmas party, I'm going to have a few and tell my boss what I really think.

Cutting the
Milk Bag

Cutting the
Milk Bag

Here's further proof that my family and I are nuts. The biggest issue in our house right now is who cuts open the next bag of milk. It's a huge deal. We're thinking of seeing a family therapist.

Years ago, it was my idea to switch to bagged milk in the first place. Bags contain the same amount of milk as cartons but take up less room in the fridge, and they're a lot cheaper. Right away it gets complicated. The milk is cheaper, but there is an initial investment. I had to buy two hard-plastic milk pitchers, and the little milk bag cutter-opener-blade thingy. They have no other name, and no other function. You must go to the store and ask, "Where do you keep those little milk bag cutter-opener-blade-thingies with the magnet thing?"

"Uh, by the milk." We had to colour coordinate the pitchers with the cutter and the fridge, a shopping nightmare. And now, when somebody finishes a bag of milk, they never want to replace it. My family will go as far as throwing out the old empty bag and placing an empty pitcher in the fridge. And when someone does cut open a new bag, it's like they've left their fingerprints. My son makes an opening the size of the hole in the Titanic. My daughter cuts a hole so small it takes twelve minutes to fill a glass. Me, of course, I do it perfectly. In my house, when you go to pour milk, it's always a surprise. We're saving money, but we need help. I think it's because packaging milk in bags just isn't right. I mean, cows don't keep milk in a . . . oh, wait, I guess they do.

Household Hints

The other day, I got a magazine at my door that had a mittful of household hints in it. It's always fascinated me how people come up with household hints in the first place. How did it ever occur to the first person that ever spilled red wine on a carpet to immediately dump salt or soda water onto it. Soda water, the freezer, and hair spray are three things that are in the household-hints hall of fame. If you think about it, if you're not spraying, you're rinsing, if you're not rinsing, you're freezing. Here are a few household hints. I'd like to know how anybody came with these.

A little spray of vodka freshens up stale dried flowers. This sounds reasonable, but remember that the suggestion comes from somebody who keeps vodka in their plant spritzer.

You will have no laundry lint if you add a cup of vinegar to your rinse cycle. Who's putting vinegar in the laundry? The person who's gooned on vodka mist, that's who.

When boiling cabbage or cauliflower, you can eliminate stinking up your kitchen by throwing one entire walnut into the water. Who thought that up? "Hey, honey, while the cabbage soup is cooking let me show you this walnut juggling trick I learned today. Whoops (plunk). Hey, the smell is gone."

I don't know how any household hints get invented. Is it that boring around the house? Do these people not have cable? Are they running around all day from room to room, spritzing vodka, throwing walnuts at stuff, and putting soda water on everything? Have they all lost their minds? Get a hobby.

The Dishwasher

The Dishwasher

There is one cupboard in our house where we keep all the dishes, glasses, cups, bowls, and flatware. It's called the dishwasher. I'm sure we have dishes that have been only in the dishwasher or on the table. They have been no where else in our house.

The most commonly heard phrase in our house used to be "How was your day?" Now, it's "Is the dishwasher clean or dirty?" We used to have one of those magnets on the dishwasher that said "clean" on one side and "dirty" on the other. But everyone in the house not only constantly forgot to run the dishwasher, they also forgot to flip the sign. You'd end up drinking juice out of yesterday's milk glass. And who needs that?

I can go back even further to a time in the history of our family when we actually used to empty the dishwasher after it ran its cycle. Those were the days, my friend. We'd have an empty dishwasher and clean dishes in the cupboard. That's all gone. Now, there's only one place for dishes in our house: the dishwasher.

As I said before, some dishes have never made it out. They keep getting passed over in favour of someone's favourite cup or glass, and they just sit there time after time, cycle after cycle, alone in the dark, getting washed and rewashed, watching their glass and ceramic friends go in and out. If it's like that in your house, try and use that lonely cup or glass or plate. Make it feel better. Let it out of its prison. After all, a dish is like a person. It just wants to go out and get dirty once in a while.

Picking Out Doorknobs

Picking Out Doorknobs

The other night, some friends of mine (and you know who you are) invited me over because they're renovating their house and they wanted me to help them pick out doorknobs. Yes, doorknobs.

Apparently they had gone through the arduous process of doorknob shopping and could not agree. They had involved professionals at different levels of doorknobbedness, and were simply not taken by any of their doorknob knowledge. I guess that would be door "knobledge."

When it comes to high-level design decisions such as doorknobs, you simply cannot involve relatives because often they have their own agenda. So they turned to me. I guess they thought, when you think of a doorknob, you think of Larry. Naturally, I was flattered. To their credit, this couple had managed, on their own, to pick out cupboard and drawer handles. But this was the next level in home-decor assistance, a much higher level. Greater concentration is required, for one must not consider only aesthetic appearance, but also ergonomics, cost of maintenance, warranty, etc. I began to feel the pressure.

The woman felt that the doorknobs should complement the light switch plates, the choosing of which apparently had been a huge discussion of its own. The man felt the knobs should blend in with the door and not stand out or match anything in particular. They had at their disposal several doorknob catalogues, and even a doorknob brochure, which had beautiful colour photos with a lovely paragraph of prose accompanying each different style of knob. Is this how Hemingway got started, writing for the doorknob brochure?

Finally, it was my turn. I had heard both sides of their story, scanned the literature, and drawn on my own expertise. I'm sure you can figure out what my advice to this couple was. "You're choosing doorknobs, for goodness sake. Doorknobs! Are you listening? Doorknobs! For the door!"

I think they took it well.

What's That Smell?

What's That Smell?

I don't know if it's safe to go back into my house. There's a smell in the kitchen. Not a good smell, but the opposite of good. Bad. A bad smell. What's worse is I don't know where it's coming from.

It started a couple of days ago. "Hey, what smells bad in the kitchen?"

"Something." What's the first thing you check? The kitchen garbage under the sink. It must go. You stick your nose in the trash, and that's not it. But it must be it. Wrap it up and take it out. Open a window. Minutes later, it's still there — the smell. Something, or someone, must have fallen behind the trash and is festering under the sink. Move the dish soap, scouring pads, Fantastik, the old bottle of silver polish I've never used — nothing. No offending odour. But somewhere in the kitchen, something evil still lurks.

This has happened before, so I go through the checklist. Maybe it's an old scouring pad? No. Does Windex go bad? No. Let's check the potato and onion drawer. One of the potatoes is bound to be brown, shrivelled, wrinkly, and smelling like Uncle Mike. No, the potatoes check out. No onions are having babies or turning into penicillin. Next, check the meat drawer in the fridge. That's been the cause before. You know, my kids have a way of opening luncheon meat, taking one piece, then hiding it under mounds of other luncheon meat until it's the same colour as the lawn. The meat is all wrapped and sealed and the best-before dates check out. Quick, a touring sniff of the rest of the fridge. It checks out, too.

The sink. I watched those ads that tell you to pour your old box of baking soda down the drain, and I thought, no, that will never happen to me. I'll bet the drain is the offender. I crane my neck, put my head into the sink — the first time I've done that sober. No, smells fine. Every cupboard, every nook, every cranny (we have one nook and six crannies) gets the sniff. Everything is pleasant, even the dishcloth. But the smell is still there. Is it coming in from the outside? Is it one of us? Quick, family, smell each other and be honest.

The only thing worse than having a bad odour mysteriously appear in your kitchen is having a bad odour mysteriously disappear from your kitchen. Whatever died in there has now mummified and will no longer be a problem. You'll find it when you move or when the painters move the stove.

But the smell is still there, like a fog, a purple haze, an omen. Or maybe it's the shoes from the hallway. I'll keep you posted.

Where Have You Lived?

Where Have You Lived?

Here's an interesting exercise you can do in the comfort of your own home, car, or when daydreaming at work. See if you can remember every place you've ever lived since you left home, home being the place where your parents let you live, the place you could go to if it all falls apart tomorrow. I mean your very own places, where you paid all or part of the rent or mortgage.

I count seventeen different places where I've parked my sorry carcass at night and said, home sweet home, baby. That's seventeen times I've rented a truck or called a moving company, seventeen times I've combed the grocery stores and trash bins of my neighbourhood looking for boxes. I've had fourteen landlords and twelve building supers, including Del, who used to sneak away from his wife and drink beer in the sauna in the basement and scare the hell out of you at ten o'clock at night. I've mailed in the change-of-address card for my driver's licence and packed up the lamp in the basement seventeen times. Seventeen different phone numbers. I remember once I had a really cool number that sounded like a business phone number. I wanted to keep it for the rest of my life but they wouldn't let me.

Seventeen places. I can remember ones I loved and ones I hated. Great views, bad views, no views, always hot, always cold, noisy, quiet, couldn't really afford it, bad roommates, good roommates, damage deposits, first and last month's rent, post-dated cheques, real estate agents, and seventeen times setting up my bed on the first night, falling into it, and saying, "I'm never doing this again."

The Suburban Experience

I've got this great idea, and it all started with farmers. When some farms couldn't make money, what did the farmers do? They opened their farms up to the city folk, and let us pay them to have the farm experience. Come ride a horse, shovel out the barn, drive a tractor, pick some apples, go for a hay ride. The list goes on. The urban crowd flocked to the farms, especially in spring and fall, and enjoyed the rural environment.

So here's where we come in. Those of us who live in houses do the same for people who live in apartments. I've lived in many apartments. Right now I live in a house. I'll probably move back into an apartment again, and I'll miss the house and yard.

Those of us who live in a house can charge people a fee to come and enjoy the house experience. Come wash your car with a hose in a driveway, $10, bring your own soap. Come rake leaves — $10 bucks for you, $5 for each kid. It costs $1 for your kid to jump around in a big pile of leaves, or three jumps for $2, the family special. I charge $1.50 to haul the trash to the curb. Cleaning the furnace costs $20. Sucking the guck out of the eaves is $1 a foot, but a family discount is available.

Have all the fun of owning a home for you and the kids without the commitment of home ownership. All the convenience of apartment dwelling, but when you feel like doing house stuff, come on over to Six Flags over Fedoruk. I can take in $100 a day in concessions alone. Pop for $1 a can and $3 for microwave pizza pops. If you're in, call me. We'll make up some flyers.

Speakers

I try to keep up with technology. But I refuse to keep up with speakers. Stereo speakers come in all shapes and sizes now. They have micro and mini speakers, and ones that fit into the wall or ceiling. Some you can paint over to disguise them, tiny speakers that make it sound like you're in a concert hall. That might be great for you, but for me, no thanks.

I need speakers, big cabinet speakers. Woofers the size of a truck tire, tweeters that can shatter a wine glass, set in huge big blocks of wood. Hundreds of trees have given their lives so that I can listen to Don Henley sing about the environment. If you hollowed out my ideal speakers, you could smuggle a family of four into the country — that's four people per channel. If you laid the speakers down on their sides and set up stools, a party of twelve could dine comfortably.

Big speakers — the kind of speakers that takes two guys to carry into a moving van, the kind that when your neighbours see movers putting them in your house, they put up a "For Sale" sign on their lawn.

"Excuse me, Larry, why do you have a fridge in your living room?"

"But that's not a fridge. That's a speaker." Richter-scale-jolting speakers. May the neighbours' windows rattle and their chimney crumble. If my speakers were outside, they would block out the sun. I want to have people over and not be able to hear the dinner conversation. When they leave, I want to put the speakers down on the floor and lie between them, turn on the stereo, and say, "Whoa."

These are the speakers I want. This is what stereo speakers should always be. But I have kids, so *they* have the good speakers. I have a really good clock radio.

Hanging
Pictures

Hanging
Pictures

Behind every perfectly hung picture in my house I've hidden at least six or eight marks, holes, chips, scuffs, or dents where I had tried to hang the picture before and just couldn't get it right. Hanging pictures is the single worst job in creating your home decor.

Couples should never hang pictures together if they want to remain a couple. I've rarely seen two people agree on whether a picture is too high, too low, over to the left, down on the left, or down on the right.

"No, more. No, less. No, *my* left." It leads to frustration, disagreements, and leaves everyone ticked off. Hanging pictures is really not good when one of the people in question possesses a hammer.

Thank goodness the majority of my pictures average 2 x 3. This gives me a six-square-foot margin of error in which to work. The small framed wall photos are a nightmare to hang. You have less than a square foot in which to hide your marks, holes, chips, scuffs, or dents from previous attempts.

I have friends who, when hanging pictures, haul out the

tape measure and pencil. That's far too scientific. If you're measuring, you have to assume that your ceiling, wall, and floor lines are straight to begin with. I don't think so. This doesn't allow for the sag quotient (SQ). Most pictures have a wire or a chain across the back. How far below the mark will the picture actually hang? It's impossible to calculate. Trial and error is the only way.

I usually just paint over existing hooks, nails, and holes, then hang the pictures there. If these spots were good enough for the previous tenant, they're good enough for me.

You can always decorate your walls with balloons instead. Just rub them on your head and stick them up! If you don't like how they look, take them off, rub the balloons some more, then put them back up. This technique doesn't work as well with pictures. Believe me, I've tried.

Time: Not the Magazine But the Non-Spatial Continuum

Shakespeare in the Park

M arch 15 is the Ides of March. What's the origin of this expression? Well, it comes from William Shakespeare. Julius Caesar was warned by a seer, or maybe some guy from Sears, to "Beware the Ides of March." Julius ignored the warning and was assassinated.

So, every year on the Ides of March, I get to thinking about Shakespeare and my annual charity work with a group I founded years ago, the Society for the Prevention of Shakespeare in the Park. The S.P.S.P. Remember, only you can prevent Shakespeare in the Park. Join the S.P.S.P. today.

Why must actors and directors force the long-winded pseudopoetic musings of an overrated writer on innocent patrons who are only out for a walk in the park? Do I go up on stage at the Old Vic and have my dog catch a frisbee? No! Do I go up on stage at Stratford and rustle up some weenies? No. Do I ride my bike or rollerblades across the stages of Broadway's finest theatres? Not lately. So why do these people insist on Shakespeare in the Park?

Remember, Shakespeare and recreation don't mix. There's no Shakespeare in the Pool Hall, no Shakespeare in the Pub. There's no Shakespeare in the Hockey Rink, and Shakespeare at the Gym went out in the seventies. So why is there Shakespeare in the Park every summer? Put Shakespeare back into stuffy old theatres where he belongs. Join the Society for the Prevention of Shakespeare in the Park. Only then can we say "All's well that ends well." All's well that ends well . . . I like how that sounds. I heard some guy in a park say it once . . .

I'm Not Happy with the Seasons

I'm not happy with the seasons. I don't like the way we've set them up, I don't like that there are four, and I don't like the order they're in.

First of all, there aren't really four seasons. There are two: summer and winter. Spring and fall are simply transitions from one real season to the other. They're not really seasons of their own. Spring is winter becoming summer, and fall is summer becoming winter. They have a little bit of each season, so we gave them a name and called them a season. That's not right. Furthermore, though fall isn't even really a season it has two names — fall and autumn. No other season has two names. How pretentious!

Second, whose idea was it to start the calendar year off with winter? Why is that a good thing? I know there's very little we can do about making January a hot, sunny, bathing-suit month in most parts of this country. We can't really change the weather. Of course, the American and Russian governments can change the weather, but they are keeping this from the public. It's part of a huge conspiracy.

Until we can change the weather, we should change the calendar year. The New Year should start on July 1. Canada Day would move to January 1. Every other holiday would remain the same. The beginning of each year would be warm. You could stay out all night and sleep under a tree. Do you see where I'm going here? Isn't it better? Trust me, it is.

We'd have to change the order of the seasons world-wide, and it certainly wouldn't do much for the people who get to live in hot, sunny climates all year round.

My Friend Lou's Birthday

My Friend Lou's Birthday

For some odd reason, yesterday I remembered that it was my friend Lou's birthday. Lou was a friend I had in high school. He was a couple of years older, but he was in the same grade. My mother wasn't crazy about Lou, but she more or less tolerated him. I haven't thought about Lou for many years, and I haven't seen or heard from him for even longer.

Lou knew how to swear in eight different languages. When Lou met someone from a different ethnic background, the first thing he did was to get them to teach him how to cuss in their mother tongue. Though he failed many subjects, he was a quick study in the salty languages.

Lou liked to give beer to his dog and cat. He could suck butane from a Bic lighter, then light it as he was exhaling so that he became a fire-breathing hoodlum. Lou knew many tricks with lighters and matches that frightened and fascinated us at the same time. He knew at least six different ways to emit disgusting sounds from his body, and could do them at will — his will, of course, not yours. The guy had his pride.

Lou could burp the alphabet (most days), and even on an off day he could burp up to the letter Q. Lou could fold paper money so that you'd see rude pictures of the queen.

When I remembered it was Lou's birthday, my first thought wasn't how old he would be, but rather, was he still alive? I hope so, because in high school we all knew a Lou. Some of us *were* Lou, some of us still are, and still others carry around a little bit of Lou in them, just for fun.

Turning Twenty Minutes
Late into Five

Yesterday I woke up twenty minutes late, yet I got to work only five minutes later than I normally do. I did this without sacrificing any of my important morning rituals — showering, shaving, drinking a beverage, and stopping to get a paper. How does this work? I'll explain it.

#1 The moment I realize I've slept in, I pop out of bed. This cuts down on lying there awake saying the daily morning mantra, "Oh god it's early, why do I have to work for a living? Oh god it's early, why do I have to work for a living? Oh god it's . . . " Not saying this saves a couple of minutes right there.

#2 I cut down on my looking-around time. No strolling over to the window, checking out the neighbourhood, doing the visual weather scan, scratching, then repeating this all over again. When I'm late, I take a quick peek. The world still exists, so I move on to the shower.

#3 I save time during my daily hygiene regimen. First, I don't play with the water to get it to just the right temperature. Close is just fine. I get in, get wet, get out. I don't wash my hair. I just wet it. It doesn't kill me. Cavemen hardly ever washed their hair. Did you ever see a bald caveman? If anything, they have great hair, thick and full. I must wash my body, but only the upper half. I let the bottom half get the soapiness of the rinse from the top half. That's good enough in an emergency.

#4 I shave quickly. Looks count, smoothness doesn't.

#5 I towel off fast. I can't afford the luxury of drying my nether regions with the hair blower.

#6 I don't pick out my clothes for the day, I just put something on. Belts and jewellery are luxuries. Forget about them for today. If I need a tie, I put one in my pocket.

#7 No coffee at home. I just grab a bottle of juice or water out of the fridge. Go, go, go! I can get coffee at work.

Trust me. I saved at least fifteen minutes. If I did this every day, even when I didn't sleep in, I'd actually be at work early. But I don't want that.

In the 'Hood

Jack and Doris

My neighbours, Jack and Doris, a kind, retired couple, have lived in the house next door since it was built, when caribou roamed freely where the convenience store now stands.

My son and I shovel their walk every once in a while and mow the patch of grass we share. One year when they grew too many tomatoes,
they would leave us one or two on our step as a thank you. Well, that's pretty neighbourly.

Well, because of their gift of the tomatoes, I've taken it upon myself to prune the trees between our yards. In return, during really bad snowfalls, he brings out his snowblower and does the walk in front of our house. Then, I shovel out the end of his driveway after the snowplow has gone by and piled up a big drift that the snowblower can't get to. Next, Jack fires up the snowblower and clears off some of my driveway. To be fair, while they were away at Christmas I cleared their entire driveway and swept their steps. As a reward, Doris gave me a jar of homemade jelly made from the berries of the trees we share (the ones I prune).

Last summer a bird got into my house and Jack got it out for me. In return, we took in their mail and watered their plants during their vacation. When they got back, we received some bedding plants and fresh baked bread.

You see what's going on. Our being neighbourly has escalated beyond belief. I think we are seconds away from doing each other's vacuuming and making meals, and before you know it, we'll all be living together.

You can choose your friends, but you can't choose your relatives or neighbours. I love Jack and Doris, but where does it end? Next week, Jack and Doris may have their own show on the radio, and I'll spend my days having coffee and volunteering down at the hospital.

I guess this is better than not being neighbourly and minding your own business. Those "minding their own business" types, they're the scary ones. They're the ones you end up talking to the duty officer about. "He always minded his own business. I never thought *this* would happen."

Oh, what the heck. Put the coffee on, Jack, I just shovelled your driveway and I'm hankerin' for some home-made jelly.

Grandma and Justin

Grandma and
Justin

A nice day in the middle of winter does wonders, and it brings out some interesting sights. Last weekend, my neighbour was babysitting her little grandson, Justin. He's about two years old, maybe two and a half. It was a warm, sunny morning, so Grandma was out on the driveway wearing a floral sweatshirt and slacks, the official uniform of grandparents everywhere. Little Justin was wearing a parka, ski pants, boots, mitts, a scarf, a toque, and sunglasses. If little Justin was going to catch anything, it wasn't going to be on Grandma's watch. After watching Grandma and Justin playing a game in the driveway, I don't think Grandma had been fully prepared to babysit Justin that day.

Grandma got two old car window scrapers — scraper on one end, brush on the other — and a tennis ball. Justin was by the garage door, and Grandma by the sidewalk. Using the scraper end she zinged one over to Justin. Thong! It hit the garage door. For six minutes Justin chased it around the driveway until the ball settled in front of his stick. He shot one over to Grandma that, even with the decline in the driveway, took about ten minutes to reach her. She shot again. Thong! It hit the garage door again. This game went back and forth all morning.

This game proved many things to me.

#1 Give a man a stick and a ball, even at a very young age, and we're good to go.

#2 Give a man a game to watch involving a stick or a ball and he'll sit there all morning. Well . . . I didn't sit there all morning . . . Okay, I did.

#3 Grandmas are very inventive.

#4 Scraper-stick ball hockey could be in the Olympics one day.

#5 A nice day in the middle of winter brings out some interesting sights.

Neighbours vs.
the Neighbourhood

I love my new neighbourhood, but I hate my new neighbours. Hate is such a strong word, but sometimes it's so appropriate.

How can I hate my neighbours and love my neighbourhood? I asked myself that same question. See, the neighbourhood is okay. It's full of nice houses and trees, and it's near stuff. It's nice to be in my neighbourhood. When you walk around my neighbourhood you get a nice feeling.

Living with my neighbours is a different deal altogether. Neighbours are not friends. The guy across the street takes the trash out wearing nothing but a towel. The guy next door runs the snow blower at 8 a.m. on Sundays. The other neighbour's cats live on my stoop. The guy two doors down, his dog, my lawn — never mind. The guy two doors the other way always wants to stop and tell me stories about his thirty-two years of driving a bus. Who does he think he is, Ralph Kramden? The other guy across the street always backs his car into the driveway crooked. He's lived in the same house for twenty-three years. Pull the car in straight!

Do I have to come over there? He's ruining the symmetry of the entire street.

These are my neighbours. I want to live down the block instead. It's the same neighbourhood, but the neighbours look better. I know that down the block they're saying the same thing. Things always look better down the block. The grass is greener down the block. Actually, the grass *is* greener. I don't know what that guy uses. I've got to ask him in the spring. I can't ask my own neighbours. I hate them.

Kids Are
People/
People
Are

Kids

Videocam

Videocam

I think I'm the only parent in my neighbourhood who doesn't have a video
camera permanently attached to my head, covering my right
eye. I know parents who have never actually seen their kids
do anything as it happened. Oh, they see it an hour later
on video tape, but never actually as it happens. They're
taping, or "filming" as many of them call it. The school
music recital looks more like the national press gallery now.
The peewee baseball game looks like a G-7 summit. The
cameras are lined up ten deep, and some days they're tiered
five high. Parents jostle for camera positions and the best
angles and zoom opportunities. I'd like to hear my son
sing in the choir, but I can't. There are too many whirring
camera noises.

I can, of course, see how you would want to save
every moment of your child's life to relive later, how bene-
ficial it would be to show videotape of your daughter as a
potato in the school play at her wedding twenty years
later. I just think that if you're going to be watching your

kids through a couple of lenses or a display screen, you might as well be watching TV.

Maybe parents are secretly hoping that they'll get a good piece of tape for those "funniest home video" or *Real TV*–type shows. Those shows always slay me. When a kid goes ass-over-tea-kettle on his bike and the parents catch it on video, you can hear the parents are laughing in the background. Put down the camera! Pick the kid up! It has to be traumatic for that kid.

I can hear these people years later, "Here's tape of my son at age one in the bath, at age five falling down in hockey, age thirteen going out on his first date, age nineteen holding up a liquor store. Well, I didn't shoot that last one. It was a gift from the police."

Kids on Leashes

You don't see many kids on leashes anymore. It used to be that at any mall or large gathering you'd see toddlers who had been harnessed by their parents. They'd attach a strap to the harness and the other end around their own wrist. The toddler had the illusion of freedom, but could always be yanked back into reality by a parent who didn't want them to wander too far. Some of the children, I think, were housebroken. Others would stop and lift their leg near a tree and you knew they'd been on the leash too long.

I never really knew how I felt about the harness-and-leash idea. The alternative, a lost child, is totally undesirable, of course. And you know kids — they have a way of disappearing into a crowd in the blink of an eye. Even the most attentive parent has lost a child, even if just for a moment. But a leash, I don't know. I can picture a leashed child lying on a therapist's couch twenty years later, moaning, "I don't know, doc. I was on a leash as a kid. The next thing I knew, I ate all my meals from a little dish on the kitchen floor, and my dad taught me how to chase a ball and bring back a stick. I had nice little squeeze toys, but then, in my teens, they had me fixed."

I never went for the leash thing when my kids were toddlers. Instead, I chose to hold their hands. I held on tight all through the mall. I'm sure each of my children has one hand smaller than the other because I held it long enough and strong enough to hinder development. I also spent a fortune on a chiropractor after carrying my kids on my shoulders through the amusement park. When they were thirteen I said enough, already. Sure, some kids are more rambunctious than others, and I guess a leash is needed. But it just seems so demeaning.

A better idea would be to leash and harness the whole family together. Everybody gets a harness and they are all attached to each other. That way, no one is on the hook, and no one gets lost. And if one leash comes off, there would be an annoying sound, like a car alarm, indicating a clasp or leash malfunction. And that way, twenty years from now, the whole family could be in therapy together.

Descendants

Descendants

Recently we did a history search on our family name. As with any family, we found some heavy hitters. Centuries ago, the Fedoruks were *some* family. I got to thinking. Centuries from now, what will our descendants have to say about *their* ancestry? I can say that I have an ancestor named Theodore, who was a member of the Roman Legion and sacrificed his life rather than denounce his faith. *My descendants will say that on graduation night my cousin Murray climbed the town water tower naked.*

I have an ancestor, Alexander, who, a hundred years ago, was vice-governor of the state and the chamberlain of the church. My descendants can look back to the 1990s at Uncle Al, who was asked to leave the Knights of Columbus, no specific reason given.

In the nineteenth century, our uncle Sergei was surgeon to the Imperial Family of Poland and professor of the Imperial Academy of Medicine. In the future, my family will say they had an Uncle Eddy who had his tonsils out and later they grew back. I have a distant cousin who, as a nobleman, signed the Polish constitution back in 1661.

Three hundred years from now, my family can look back at a distant cousin who knew how to sign his mother's name on a cheque. I'm telling you, family trees just aren't what they used to be.

And I'll bet it's not just my family. I'll bet you that families everywhere look back through the centuries when the family tree sprang forth like the mighty oak. Now, we have to call the family-tree guy to spray for bugs.

To Be a Giant

When I was a kid I wanted to be a giant. I think we all did. I don't mean that I wanted to be the kind of giant that has to duck walking through doorways, and has a hard time finding pants to fit, a "my, but your son is tall" giant. I didn't want to be your run-of-the-mill seven-foot giant. I wanted to be a sixty- to eighty-foot giant. A huge, freakazoid, rule-the-world giant, that's what I wanted to be.

I wanted to put my foot down beside the little chair, the rocking chair, and the other chair for two people to curl up in, just like the Friendly Giant did. You'd have to look up, way up. I wouldn't have had a pet rooster named Rusty. I wouldn't even have had a pet rooster because I'd be a giant. (Jerome must have been a huge, steroid-freak giraffe. There's no way he was the size of a normal giraffe. He was as tall as Friendly.) I would have eaten chickens like jelly beans, popping them in my mouth until I was full.

Because of Friendly, and Gulliver, and "Jack and the Beanstalk", and *The Twilight Zone*, and even King Kong, I always thought it would be cool to be a giant. It'd be cool to climb skyscrapers and play with toy cars (except they'd be normal cars and people would freak), but I wouldn't hurt anybody, unless if I got fired for no good reason. Then I might step on my boss's house or something, then on my boss.

My crushing would always be for the good of humankind. People wouldn't realize that at first and they'd fire weapons at me. The bullets and missiles would feel like mosquitoes biting me, but eventually I'd pass out from too many hits. People would be mad at me until they figured out that I was only trying to do good and I was lonely. I was lonely because there was no giant woman. Who could love me?

That's really why I never became a giant. There wasn't a future in it.

Work, Work
Work, That's
All I
Ever

Do

Robots

Robots

If you don't mind my saying so, you scientists are really falling behind on your robot work. Day to day, I'm on the bus, I'm in the store, I'm here, I'm there, and frankly, I don't see a lot of robots around. Over the course of a week, I may see one, two at the most.

As a child, television, books, and the movies led me to believe that by the 1990s there would be a whole society of robots rolling around doing all the stuff we humans hate to do. Sure, we have computers that play chess, and little remote-control R2D2s that the bomb squad sends in. But I'm talking about a full-blown, full-grown, "Danger, danger, Will Robinson" mechanical marvel that the family becomes attached to, and that falls in love with a Pepsi machine, which everyone thinks is so cute. That's the kind of robot I want in society. As a kid, that was the kind of robot I was promised by the year 2000.

I don't think we're even close to having robots like that. (Big machines with midgets at the bottom pedalling around don't count, though it would be a start.) If scientists were to put away all the work they're doing on stomach crunchers, sandwich makers, and every other device you see on infomercials, and make us a good robot, I think we'd be ahead. Would humans lose jobs? Some would, yes, but a whole robot market would open up: manufacturing, sales, repair, and accessories. I want to be able to go to a Robots R Us or a Robot Shack and get me a robot. And I want it by the year 2000.

We're nearly at the millennium. You don't have many weeks left, scientists of the world. I've got comic books I can lend you if you need a place to start.

White Coat Work

It may be a little late for me to switch careers, but I still want a job that involves wearing a white coat. To me, nothing elevates the status of an occupation more than if you have to wear a white coat while performing your duties.

A white coat gives you so much authority. Lots of people have to wear white coats on the job. Doctors do, and so do people in doctor-related jobs. Pharmacists wear white coats, and so does the lady at the drugstore make-up counter. Manicurists and butchers wear white coats. (Butchers' coats are usually more bloody than manicurists', unless the manicurist is really bad.) Scientists and people who work in labs wear white coats. They're called "lab coats." I imagine that if you were a white coat salesperson, you would have to wear one to show off your product.

A white coat makes you look like you really know what you're doing. If I had some kind of an attack in the middle of the sidewalk and a person in a white coat showed up to treat me, I'd let them do anything to me.

"I think it's my appendix. It's gotta come out. Now!"

"But I'm a manicurist!" they would say.

"I don't care. Just do it!"

I don't know if it would work the other way around. You wouldn't ask your doctor for make-up tips just because she was wearing a white coat.

I think every workplace, regardless of what kind of work is done, should own one white coat. Each employee should get a turn wearing it for a day or a week. That person would be called a "technical supervisor," or a "lab chief," and all week they would walk around looking smug performing white coat jobs around the office, such as doing people's nails.

Recognized by Occupation

I'm amazed at the number of people we introduce and recognize by their occupation. "Hey, this is my friend, the accountant." "This is Tom, the doctor I told you about." "Oh, I remember you. You're that policeman friend of Janice's." In some cases, you're identified by your work more than by your name or the kind of person you are. You become known for what you do.

You take on everything that everyone in that profession has done before you. You hear statements like, "What do you expect from Dave? He's an actor." And, "Of course, Ed's a lawyer. Now it makes sense."

I think that being known by what you do is more common in the more specialized and high profile jobs. I don't think that's right. You should be able to work a person's occupation into any introduction. "Hey, everyone, this is George, that pipefitter I was mentioning." "Al, aren't you the duct cleaner I met at that party?" "I don't remember your name, but you're an assistant produce manager, aren't you?"

Either we do it for everyone or we do it for no one. It'd be easier not to do it for anybody. We should stick to using people's names because if we mentioned occupations for everyone we'd have to say things like, "This is my friend Barry. He sits at the window and looks at cars." "This is Chuck. He spends all day in an office covering his butt." "You all remember Bill. He's a burden on society."

Remembering Names

There are people out there who can't remember other people's names. I'll be honest — I'm one of those people. I've known my kids for years, but every once in a while they have to wear name tags to help me out.

I can meet someone socially and have a long conversation with them, but two minutes later I can't remember their name. It's gone from my mind, never to return. When that happens, I have to slink up to a mutual friend and say, "That guy over there, what's his name again? Right. Thanks." As I'm walking away, I forget it again. The odd thing is, I can usually remember just about everything else about them. Six months later I can remember that you told me you rented a grey Lincoln for your youngest sister's wedding, but your name . . . Ray, Mort, Sanji . . . I don't know. Sorry.

There are memory tricks and other methods, and then there's that guy on television who guarantees you a better memory. What's his name? There's the old trick where you ask the person their name and when they say, "Bob," you say, "No, I remember that Bob's your first name. I was wondering about your *last* name," or vice versa. That's a clever trick, but transparent.

How important is a name, really? I can remember some pretty cool stuff you told me. What does it matter that I can't remember your name? You probably didn't even get to choose it.

What I don't do is what certain people do when they can't remember *my* name. They say to me, "Hey, how's it going, big guy?" Or, "Haven't seen you in a while, pal." Then there's "What's new, chief?" At first I thought "big guy" was a term of male affection, but then I heard the same person who called me that call *another* man "big guy." I was hurt.

"Hey, I thought *I* was 'big guy'. Apparently I'm not your only 'chief' either." Look, I really don't care that you don't remember my name, but I'm not your 'big guy,' okay, pal?

Hobbies
Hobbies

I was helping my son fill out a job application form the other day (I'm so good with forms), and we got to the bottom part where it said, "Hobbies."

"What are my hobbies, Dad? Do I have hobbies? What should I put down for hobbies? What *are* hobbies?"

Those are all good questions. I'm not sure that hobbies exist anymore. My son and I couldn't write down "sports" or "interests," because those went under their own headings.

"Well, son, do you collect anything besides dust?"

"No."

"Do you like to build anything?"

"No."

"Do you paint, sculpt, work in the garden?"

"Does mowing the lawn count?"

"Why do you ask? You don't cut the lawn. Regardless, it doesn't count."

"Then, no. No hobbies. What are your hobbies, Dad? I'll just fill in your hobbies."

"Same as you. None."

It's 1998. I have a job, a home, and kids. Who has time for model trains? That's what hobbies mean to me — model trains, model cars, collecting stamps, collecting anything, gardening, painting, and sculpting. Reading is borderline. If all you read is the *National Enquirer* and your Visa statement, reading doesn't stand up as a hobby. Neither does watching TV or playing the lotto.

My conclusion is "hobby" is an outdated word. Living, that's my hobby. Life itself.

By the way, the preceding few paragraphs are what I wrote down on my son's application form under "hobbies." Let them chew on that a while. I'm sure he'll get the job.

Miscellaneous:

When Etc.

Just Won't

Do

What's New?

The worst question anybody can ask you, a question for which you never have a good answer, is "What's new?" God, I hate that question. Why? Because I never have a good answer. Nothing much is ever new.

The person who asks me "What's new?" has just reminded me that my life is day-to-day ongoing drudgery, a mindless routine, repetition and routine, and repetition. But when your life does have new things in it, a house, a car, a new baby, people never seem to ask you that question. Of course not. They wait until your life returns to the daily routine, the repetition and routine, and repetition, and then they say, "Oh, hi, Larry, what's new?"

Sure, maybe one day I'll be wearing new clothes, but you can't answer, "Well, my pants, that's what's new. My pants, my pants are new. I have new pants."

When someone asks, "What's new?" we usually reply, "Nothing much," or "You know, same old, same old." (We repeat "same old" to emphasize that our life is routine, repetition and routine, and repetition.) Sometimes we say,

"Same stuff, different day" (only we don't say "stuff"). That means we're boring, but we're still cool.

I think all we need to do is to come up with a series of new snappy retorts to that question.

"Hey man, long time no see, what's new?"

"That greeting sure isn't." "What's new? Not much. Just my left kidney." "Tomorrow is a new day dawning." Maybe we shouldn't use that last one. Or we could answer, "I knew you'd be asking that question, so I prepared a brief synopsis since the last time I saw you. Let me read it aloud." Maybe then, at least, people will stop asking that question.

Packing

I have to fly soon. I haven't flown in a while. I don't really fly that often, so I'm stressed about packing. I'm the world's worst packer. Normally, if I'm going away for a day or even a month, my idea of packing is to jam everything I own into a couple of suitcases and take it all with me. That way I won't forget anything. I always have the two largest, heaviest suitcases, and a jam-packed carry-on that actually slows down the X-ray conveyor belt. Once, the belt actually seized up from the weight of my luggage. People are always shocked at the amount of stuff I'm bringing. They fear that I'm going to stay for six months because of the amount of luggage I have.

It's amazing to me that when I'm at home I can live in the same pair of sweatpants and T-shirt for forty-eight hours, but for a weekend away I need two suits, all my ties, fourteen pairs of underwear, an entire sock drawer, a few pairs of jeans, some sweatshirts, three regular shirts, eight pairs of shoes, and eleven belts. It's people like me who end up buying motor homes. We are just so stressed out over not having our stuff with us, we end up buying a house on wheels. Believe me, if I could pack my stove, fridge, microwave, and VCR for a weekend away, I would. If the airplane limit was two bags *and* two appliances, I'd be a lot happier about travelling.

I'm trying to get better at packing. I try to plan which clothes I'll need, which socks, which watch, which belt. Just the bare minimum. The efficient traveller. Oh, who am I kidding? Has anybody got a Winnebago I can borrow for the weekend?

Interventions

Interventions

Have you ever heard of an intervention? You hear about celebrity interventions all the time. A person has trouble coping, so they use drugs or drink alcohol. They can't be helped until they are ready to help themselves, but often it's too late for that, so a group of the person's friends get together and stage an intervention. They confront the person, intervene, express their concern, and force the person to see what they're doing to themselves and to others. They offer help to turn the person around. An intervention. I'm all for it, or anything that helps.

Would interventions work in other areas of life? Why not? If this thing works for drugs and alcohol, let's try it for other problems. How about a clothing intervention? "Hey, Bob, we really don't like what you've been wearing around the office lately. You look geeky, and make us feel like we work in a geek factory. We can't hear over your shirt. Turn it down a notch or two, would ya?"

How about a manners intervention? "Chuck, all of us got together and we're really concerned. We think you're a Neanderthal. None of us is your "baby," so don't call us that. And, yes, in some countries burping after a meal *is* a compliment, but this is not one of those countries. It's just an intervention, Chuck, it's nothing personal."

A hair intervention. "Diane, what's with the hair lately?" "Raymond. The rug. Not fooling anybody."

How about make-up? "Hello, Yolanda, we're holding an intervention to demand you give up your putty knife." Cleanliness. "Paul, sorry to intervene, but for god's sake . . . "

Driving. "Excuse me, pal, does this model not come with a signal light? Can't you see what you're doing to yourself and to those around you?"

If you're just nosy and catty, no one wants to hear about it. But call it an intervention and, well, you're just looking out for the welfare of the people around you.

Oh, one more. How about a nutshell intervention? "Larry, excuse me . . . you're starting to babble."

Carry-on Luggage

What has happened to carry-on luggage? Has it grown, or have I gotten smaller? Remember when carry-on luggage used to be called a "flight bag"? Often flight bags were given as gifts by the airline. "Thank you for flying the friendly skies. Here are your tickets and a complimentary flight bag. You can use it for your carry-on." What handsome blue square nylon bags they were, with the airline's logo proudly displayed. You almost felt like one of the crew. But those days are gone.

The blue square nylon bag was designed to fit neatly under the seat, or snuggly in the overhead compartment. But now that those days are behind us, the words "carry-on luggage" are open to each passenger's own interpretation. Most people think, if I can carry it, and they let me on, it's carry-on.

"I have the box from my 48" TV filled with canned goods and some pewter sculptures. I've tied it haphazardly with twine. This is my carry-on."

"Here's a suitcase the size of a riding mower. I'm too 'busy' to wait at the luggage carousel with the rest of you suckers, so I'm going to carry it on, and who's going to stop me?" Usually, no one. When you get to your destination, why bother renting a car? I'm sure they'd let you bring your Geo along as a carry-on. It doesn't quite fit under the seat or in the overhead, but never mind. They'll find a place for it.

The biggest carry-on scam is the suit bag. Those button-down-collar types in business class who travel often and can't be bothered waiting around, bring their garment bag on the airplane. "Hang this up for me, will you, dear?" If they carried only one suit I wouldn't mind. But they have three changes of clothes and four litres of scotch in there. If the suit in the bag's anything like the suit they're wearing, they needn't bother hanging it up. If it was me, I'd hang it from the wing and hope to lose it over Cleveland.

Why do women get to bring a purse *and* a carry-on? It wouldn't be so bad, except a traveller's purse is usually big enough to hold two small children.

It's time to bring back the little blue square nylon flight bag. Or else, if your carry-on doesn't fit under the seat, then it rides *in* the seat and *you* get stuffed under the seat or in the overhead.

Time To Rename Canada

Canada needs a name change. When you watch the Olympics, all these countries have new names, and then there's Canada — same old name. People say Canada wouldn't be Canada without Quebec. Personally, I want Quebec to stay, but on the other hand, let them go and just change the name of our country. Bangladesh did it. So did Myanmar and Yugoslavia. Zaire did it twice.

I like the name Doug. Doug would be a good name for this country. If a country can be named Chad, then a country can be named Doug. I live in the country of Doug. "O Doug! Our home and native land . . ." The only thing wrong with that is then people would call our country "Dougie." I don't like that.

Doug's a man's name, and it's not very ethnic. Canada has a rich ethnic mix. But we couldn't call the country Stanislav or Vijay because then someone would be ticked off. How about we just go by "the former Canada." That would work until we came up with a new name. Or maybe we could take on a sponsor. One year our country could be called "Nike," the next year "Goodyear," the next year the "Dominion of Superfresh." You could charge more for a sponsorship in an Olympic year.

"Hey there's Jean Chretien, he's prime minister of the new Chevrolet Lumina." It's like when your parents name you. You have no say in the matter. At least when you're older you can go by your middle name, or a nickname, or initials. I had no say in the naming of Canada, and I'd like a say. The fairest thing to do would be to hold a lottery. Everyone in Canada gets to put their name into a hat (a really big hat), then once a year we'd draw a name and that would be the name of the nation for a year. The country could even be named after you. Anything but Canada. Love the country, hate the name.

Prostate, Prostrate

Do you ever confuse two similar words in the English language? You're a reasonably intelligent person with a fair grasp of the language, yet two similar words boggle the heck out of you. The two I always confuse are "prostrate" and "prostate."

I know that a prostate is a gland. Men have a prostate. Prostrate means to lie down low or flat in an act of submission or humility. You lie prone . . . or is that prune? No, prunes help your prostate. Not to be confused with pone, which is corn bread, and doesn't go well with prunes.

I know the difference between prostate and prostrate, yet to call up either word in a conversation befuddles me. "Oh yes, my neighbour Carl just had prostrate surgery."

"Prostrate? Don't you mean prostate?"

"Uh, no. No I don't. He had surgery lying face down. As a matter of fact, I'm not a doctor, but I think you have to have prostate surgery prostrate." Good. I avoided that social faux pas.

"The other day, I walk into the house in the middle of the day and my son's prostate on the couch."

"What? His gland was there right on the sofa? Did it fall out? Did he not notice it there? Did he just leave it there? Did he forget it?"

"Did I say prostate? I meant Pro State. It's a big college in the U.S. He's thinking of going." Wow, another quick tap dance fixes that one.

I know the difference. Prostate, gland; prostrate, lying down. Gland, down, gland, down, gland, down. For some reason, in day-to-day use I find it very infusing.

Obscenities All in a Row

I was standing in line for something at the mall on the weekend, and struck up a conversation with a guy whose every second word was an obscenity. Often, it was the same obscenity used in different ways. This guy was impressive. I thought I'd heard almost every use of the darker side of our language, but this guy was good. And I should also say that every second word was only an average. Sometimes he would go three or four words without uttering an off-colour remark, and sometimes he could string three or four obscenities together to form a sentence all of their own. He was impressive. If only he could channel his creativity for good instead of evil.

But there he was, striking up a conversation with me, a total stranger, and he didn't hold back at all. The racier words he used as nouns, verbs, adjectives, and adverbs. He said them at the end of sentences, at the beginning, in the middle of existing words — the whole gamut. I thought of objecting, but truthfully, I was somewhat frightened. I didn't want any of this barrage directed at me. I just smiled, and nodded like an idiot.

I know the mall on a Christmas shopping weekend can bring out the worst in any of us, but this guy wasn't new to sweardom. He was a seasoned pro. You could tell. He'd been working on his banter for years. It was flawless, seamless. Other than the fact that these words are deemed unacceptable by the masses, it was a literary work of art. Some guys would be very offensive with this kind of talk, but this guy — I don't know whether it was his age or what — he just seemed colourful. Colourful? Hell, he was a bloody kaleidoscope. Somehow, obscenities and all, he made it work. Well, except for one. That word kind of doesn't fit between the words "Merry" and "Christmas." Sir, if you don't mind, I hear ya, but please. Thanks anyway, for the greeting.

Umbrellas

Umbrellas are the absolute worst. It's almost better to get soaking wet.

First of all, when it's raining and you're at home, you've left your umbrella at work. When it's raining and you're at work, your umbrella's at home. Many people buy two or three umbrellas, the cheap ones, so they have one everywhere. Those umbrellas are a rip-off. One gust of wind, and you're carrying an inverted cone that collects water. Invariably, one or two of the sections come apart and just hang there. You see people walking in the rain, trying to manoeuvre the umbrella so that they are under the only part that's still attached. Those are the little cheap ones you see abandoned at the bus stop after a particularly heavy rain. Some of them are just skeletons, barely recognizable. The umbrella coroner has to come along and identify the remains. There's $4.95 well spent.

Some people spend $20 to $60 on a really good umbrella that'll withstand anything. Those are the ones you tend to leave on the bus. If you find a good one, you turn it in to the lost and found. Not bloody likely. Golf umbrellas are good, but they take up an entire city sidewalk. Sure you're dry, but someone else will lose an eye. And what do you do with a soaking wet umbrella? You can't open it up to dry inside, that's bad luck. Everybody knows that.

I can't think of anything good about umbrellas at all. I think we'd all be better off taking baths in Scotchgard. Scotchgard your entire body, then watch the water bead up and roll off your skin and hair and clothes. Problem solved. You'll never need another umbrella as long as you live.

What Is Life?

This Is Life

Do you know what life is? I'll tell you what life is. A lot of people never discover the secret of life. I did. It's your lucky day. Now I'll share it with you.

Life is a bunch of little things. That's it. Don't thank me just yet.

People are led to believe that life is a bunch of big things — weddings, funerals, jobs, children. No, life's none of those things.

Sure, you can meet the right person, fall in love, and get married. No big deal. But how are you going to get to the wedding if you've locked your keys in your car? That's a little thing. It drives you crazy.

Sure, you've got a big report due at work the next day, but if you feel like corn flakes and there's no milk in the house, how can you be expected to function?

Life is simply one little thing after another. You're all psyched to wear the brown shirt with the stripes but it's in the laundry. Your day is shot, possibly your whole week. Maybe your RSPs are taking a beating, and your bank is calling, but what's really bugging you is that you want to rent *Jerry Maguire* and it's out, again.

Little things. That's life. It's that simple. So if you're sitting there thinking, "Oh, my heart, my head, my soul, why are we here, what's next, what should I do?" and the dishwasher melts your Tupperware, look to the Tupperware, my friend. *That's* life.